CW01640859

ENGAGING WITH AQA GCSE (9–1) History

ELIZABETHAN ENGLAND c1568–1603

BRITISH DEPTH STUDY

DALE BANHAM

HODDER EDUCATION
AN HACHETTE UK COMPANY

The Publishers would like to thank the following for permission to reproduce copyright material.

Photo credits

p.6 © GL Archive/Alamy Stock Photo; **p.7** *tl* © Granger Historical Picture Archive/Alamy Stock Photo; *tc* © The British Library Board/public domain; *tr* © Ian Dagnall/Alamy Stock Photo; *bl* © Classic Image/Alamy Stock Photo; *bc* © Pictorial Press Ltd/Alamy Stock Photo; *br* © Alto Vintage Images/Alamy Stock Photo; **p.10** © GL Archive/Alamy Stock Photo; **p.16** *l* © The Print Collector/Alamy Stock Photo; *r* © Granger Historical Picture Archive/Alamy Stock Photo; **p.17** *l* © Classic Image/Alamy Stock Photo; *r* © IanDagnall Computing/Alamy Stock Photo; **p.19** *l* © Photo 12/Alamy Stock Photo; *r* © IanDagnall Computing/Alamy Stock Photo; **p.20** © IanDagnall Computing/Alamy Stock Photo; **p.22** © The Print Collector/Alamy Stock Photo; **p.26** © Heritage Image Partnership Ltd/Alamy Stock Photo; **p.27** © Historic England Archive; **p.28** IanDagnall Computing/Alamy Stock Photo; **p.31** © Look and Learn; **p.32** © Granger Historical Picture Archive/Alamy Stock Photo; **p.35** © mary416 - stock.adobe.com; **p.36** © The National Trust Photolibrary/Alamy Stock Photo; **p.38–39** Library of Congress Prints and Photographs Division/LC-DIG-pga-02965; **p.42** © Look and Learn/Peter Jackson Collection/Bridgeman Images; **p.46** © The British Library Board/public domain; **p.49** © Fotosearch/Getty Images; **p.52** © Ian Dagnall/Alamy Stock Photo; **p.58** © World History Archive/Alamy Stock Photo; **p.60–61** © DeAgostini/Getty Images; **p.63** © Look and Learn; **p.64** © Classic Image/Alamy Stock Photo; **p.70** © Bridgeman Images; **p.73** © Bridgeman Images; **p.75** © Chronicle/Alamy Stock Photo; **p.76** © Pictorial Press Ltd/Alamy Stock Photo; **p.79** © Heritage Image Partnership Ltd/Alamy Stock Photo; **p.80** © Granger Historical Picture Archive/Alamy Stock Photo; **p.82** © Alto Vintage Images/Alamy Stock Photo; **p.90** Library of Congress, Rare Book & Special Collections Division; **p.92** © Classic Image/Alamy Stock Photo.

Acknowledgements

p.89 'The Spanish Armada: all at sea' by Dan Snow, History Extra, April 23, 2005, © Immediate Media Company Ltd 2019. Retrieved from https://www.historyextra.com/period/elizabethan/the-spanish-armada-all-at-sea/; **p.93** 'The Spanish Armada: England's lucky escape' by Robert Hutchinson, History Extra, April 29, 2013, © Immediate Media Company Ltd 2019. Retrieved from https://www.historyextra.com/period/tudor/the-spanish-armada-englands-lucky-escape/

Note: The wording and sentence structure of some written sources have been adapted and simplified to make them accessible to all pupils while faithfully preserving the sense of the originals.

Orders: please contact Hachette UK Distribution, Hely Hutchinson Centre, Milton Road, Didcot, Oxfordshire, OX11 7HH.
Telephone: +44 (0)1235 827827. Email education@hachette.co.uk. Lines are open from 9 a.m. to 5 p.m., Monday to Friday.
You can also order through our website: www.hoddereducation.com

ISBN: 978 1 5104 5894 9

First published in 2020 by
Hodder Education,
An Hachette UK Company
Carmelite House
50 Victoria Embankment
London EC4Y 0DZ

www.hoddereducation.co.uk

Impression number 10 9 8 7 6 5

Year 2024 2023

Cover photo © Heritage Image Partnership Ltd/Alamy Stock Photo

Illustrations by D'AVILA Illustration Agency and Aptara

Typeset by Aptara

Printed and bound by CPI Group (UK) Ltd, Croydon, CR0 4YY

A catalogue record for this title is available from the British Library.

CONTENTS

0.1 Your exam: What is assessed and how

The GCSE course that you are following is made up of four different studies.

	Paper 1: Understanding the modern world	Paper 2: Shaping the nation
What is assessed?	**Section A: Period study** This focuses on key developments in a country's history over at least a 50-year period	**Section A: Thematic study** This looks at key developments in Britain over a long period of time (at least 800 years)
	Section B: Wider world depth study This focuses on international conflict and tension over a period of 20–25 years	**Section B: British depth study including the historic environment** This focuses on a period of British history over a short period of time (under 40 years) and includes the study of a specific historic environment
How is it assessed?	Written exam: 2 hours 50% of your GCSE (84 marks) Section A – 6 compulsory questions (40 marks) Section B – 4 compulsory questions (40 marks plus 4 marks for spelling, punctuation and grammar)	Written exam: 2 hours 50% of your GCSE (84 marks) Section A – 4 compulsory questions (40 marks plus 4 marks for spelling, punctuation and grammar) **Section B – 4 compulsory questions (40 marks) (see opposite)**

This book prepares you for the British Depth Study: **Elizabethan England, c1568–1603**.

It focuses on the last 35 years of Elizabeth's reign. You will study:

- the major events of Elizabeth's reign
- political, economic, religious, social and cultural developments.

Part	Key content (topics)	Review pages
Part 1: Elizabeth I's court and parliament	**1** Elizabeth I and her court **2** The difficulties of a female ruler	Pages 10–31
Part 2: Life in Elizabethan times	**3** A 'Golden Age' **4** The poor **5** English sailors	Pages 32–63
Part 3: Troubles at home and abroad	**6** Religious matters **7** Mary Queen of Scots **8** The conflict with Spain	Pages 64–93

Revision Tip

Break down your revision into manageable chunks of content

This book is organised into the three parts and the eight topics of the specification. At the end of each part of the course, make sure you review and revise what you have just covered. The 'Exam Practice', 'Recall Challenge' and 'Review' features will help you to do this.

How the British Depth Study will be examined

You will be examined on your knowledge and understanding of the British Depth Study in Paper 2.

The table below shows the type of questions you will be asked. You should always spend a couple of minutes making sure you identify the focus of the question and planning your approach before you start to write your answer. This book will give you step-by-step guidance on how to tackle each type of question.

Type of question		Guidance	Marks	Writing time	Advice and practice
1	How convincing is Interpretation A about …	Base your evaluation on the content of the interpretation. Identify the point/view/argument being made in the interpretation about the given issue in the question. Then, use your knowledge and understanding of the period to evaluate how convincing this interpretation is. How far does it match your contextual knowledge of the period?	8	10 minutes	Pages 31, 63, 89, 93
2	Explain what was important about …	Focus on the idea of importance. Aim to identify two main ways in which the event/development/issue in the question was important. What impact did it have at the time? Support each of the points you make with examples/evidence **and** explain why this led to important changes/problems/developments.	8	10 minutes	Pages 15, 31, 63, 81, 93
3	Write an account of …	Make sure you identify the focus of the question – it could ask you to write an account of how an issue/development affected the country (in a positive or negative way). Aim to identify and explain two ways in which the given event or issue led to problems/benefits for the country.	8	10 minutes	Pages 31, 51, 73, 93
4	The Historic Environment question	This is an essay question, requiring you to reach a **judgement** about a statement provided in the question. Aim to evaluate the point/view/argument stated in the question first. Weigh how important it was compared to **two** other factors/reasons/changes. Reach a judgement – was it the most important factor/reason/change? Use your knowledge of wider events and developments to reach a judgement.	16	20 minutes	Pages 45, 91, 93

Revision Tips

Make exam practice part of your revision

Exam Tips give you step-by-step guidance on how to tackle each type of question. Effective revision is not just learning the content. You need to understand what each type of question is asking you to think about in the exam and to practise delivering it.

Take responsibility

Reflect on your strengths and weaknesses. What question types do you struggle with? Take responsibility: spend more time practising the types of question you find most difficult. Use feedback from your teacher to improve your approach.

0.2 The Big Picture: Identify the key questions

Reflect

The following summaries identify the people, key events and big questions that this course will cover. However, top history students also ask questions of their own! As you read the summary of each topic, note down your own questions (large or small) about it. Also, make a note of the key words and individuals in bold. You will be quizzed on how much you can remember about them on page 9.

Summarise

Throughout this book you will be encouraged to develop memory aids to help you recall important information and ideas. Look at the acronym opposite which shows problems Elizabeth faced. Copy and complete the memory aid by adding examples from 'The Big Picture' of each problem.

Political problems *e.g. rebellions led by leading nobles such as the Duke of Norfolk*
Economic problems *e.g. increasing…*
Religious problems *e.g. disagreements between…*
Military problems *e.g. invasion by…*
Succession problems *e.g. arguments over…*

PART 1: Elizabeth I's court and parliament

Topic 1: Elizabeth I and her court

Elizabeth had a difficult childhood. Her mother was executed on the orders of her father, Henry VIII, when she was only three years old. Elizabeth became Queen when her half-sister, Mary I, died in 1558.

Elizabeth was expected to govern the country and make all the important decisions. The **Privy Council**, a small group of key **ministers**, advised the Queen and helped her run the country.

Elizabeth also needed the support of the **nobles**, rich and powerful landowners who might rebel against the Queen if they were unhappy. Through a system of **patronage**, Elizabeth rewarded loyal nobles with important positions in the government.

Big question: How did Elizabeth rule the country?

Topic 2: The difficulties of a female ruler

Some claimed that females could not rule effectively. Many **Catholics** challenged Elizabeth's right to rule. They refused to recognise her father's marriage to Anne Boleyn.

Parliament was not as powerful as it is today, but it still challenged Elizabeth on issues such as religion and put pressure on her to marry. They were worried about the **succession** (who would rule the country when Elizabeth died).

Elizabeth also faced challenges from some leading nobles. In 1571, the Duke of Norfolk (pictured) plotted to overthrow Elizabeth. The Earl of Essex led a rebellion against her in 1601.

Big question: What challenges did Elizabeth face?

PART 2: Life in Elizabethan times

Topic 3: A 'Golden Age'

Living standards improved for the **gentry** (landowners below the rank of nobles). Members of the gentry such as Bess of Hardwick (pictured), showed their wealth and status by building great country houses, decorated with the latest fashions.

London became an important centre for trade. The city's merchants became very wealthy. Many theatres were built to entertain the growing population and the plays of William Shakespeare became popular.

Big question:
Why has Elizabeth's reign been seen as a Golden Age?

Topic 4: The poor

Life in Elizabethan times did not improve for everyone. Rising unemployment led to increased **poverty**. Local councils and Elizabeth's government passed some laws to help poor people, but beggars were harshly punished. Thomas Harman produced a book (see picture) that warned people about **vagabonds** (homeless people who roamed the country looking for work). He claimed they would try to cheat people out of money.

Big question:
How did people respond to poverty?

Topic 5: English sailors

English sailors set off on expeditions, setting up trade links that would later lead to the establishment of a British **Empire**. John Hawkins (pictured) made trips to West Africa where he took local people from their homes. He then sailed across the Atlantic and sold the people into slavery in Spanish colonies in the West Indies (Caribbean). Francis Drake became famous for his **circumnavigation** of the globe, becoming the first Englishman to travel all the way round the circumference of the world. Walter Raleigh organised expeditions to North America.

Big question:
Why were the voyages of exploration and colonisation important?

PART 3: Troubles at home and abroad

Topic 6: Religious matters

After Queen Mary's failed attempt to bring back Catholicism, Elizabeth established a Protestant Church of England. This led to her **excommunication** – which means the Pope expelled her from the Catholic church and encouraged Catholics to rebel against her. Catholic **missionaries** started to secretly arrive in England. Their aim was to spread the Catholic religion. In response, Elizabeth's government introduced strict laws against Catholics and Francis Walsingham (pictured) established a spy network to uncover Catholic plots against Elizabeth.

Big question:
Why did religious matters create trouble for Elizabeth?

Topic 7: Mary Queen of Scots

The arrival of Mary Queen of Scots (pictured) in England created a major problem for Elizabeth. She was Elizabeth's cousin and had a strong claim to the English throne, but she was also a Catholic. Protestant, Scottish nobles had rebelled against Mary and forced her to flee to England. Despite being imprisoned, Mary became involved in plots to overthrow Elizabeth. She was executed in 1587 after Elizabeth reluctantly agreed to sign her death warrant.

Big question:
What problems did the arrival of Mary Queen of Scots create for Elizabeth?

Topic 8: The conflict with Spain

Conflict developed between England and Spain when English sailors attacked Spanish treasure ships and Elizabeth started to support people in the Netherlands who were rebelling against Spanish rule. Philip II (pictured), the King of Spain, sent a large **armada** to invade England. Some historians argue that it was defeated due to clever English tactics or better designed English ships. Others argue that the Spanish made mistakes or that the weather played a key role in deciding the outcome.

Big question:
Why was the Spanish Armada defeated?

0.3 Key features: How this book works

The tasks in this book will help you learn what you need to know and how to apply your knowledge to answer exam questions effectively. They are your '**Steps to success**'.

Research & Record

Gets the **learning** into your head in the first place and into your notebook. Starts you thinking in a way that will help you produce good answers to the exam questions.

Each **research question** reflects an issue that the examiners will expect you to be expert on. Complete these tasks, which build an answer to each research question, carefully and neatly because they will become your revision notes. Many tasks use tables. Give yourself room – each table should have its own page.

If you have gaps in your knowledge, go back to your research notes and the relevant section of this book and make sure that you add anything that is missing so you have covered all the key topics in enough detail.

Summarise

Turns your learning into a **memorable form**. Sometimes we guide you to do this, but mostly it is up to you.

Memory aids are different from your research notes. They use images or diagrams, but very few words. Most people remember better if something is summarised with both text and visuals.

If you cannot remember some of the content you have covered, go back to your research notes and improve or recreate your memory aid.

Reflect

Makes you form **connections** between what you have already learnt and what you are about to learn.

Apply ▶ Recall Challenge

Prepares you for exams by helping you to test yourself on what you have learnt.

Quizzes, games and competitions test how much you can remember. They identify your weak spots where you need to spend more time.

Apply ▶ Exam Practice

Continues to prepare you for the exam by answering exam-style questions with our Exam Tips to guide you.

Our **practice questions** are like the questions you will be asked in the exam, although none of them come from actual past papers. You can get real papers from your teacher or from the AQA website. There are **Exam Tips** for each question type – showing you how to approach it.

If you did not understand how to approach a question, go back to the Exam Tips in this book and re-read them, checking you fully understand what is required in a good answer to that type of question.

Review

Reviews the **big ideas and concepts**. We also encourage you to **review your own learning**.

Take responsibility
Review your own learning. What areas did you do well on? What areas do you need to improve?

Revision Tips

1 **Don't delay revision until just before the exam**
Revision should be an ongoing process. You need to revisit topics that you have studied regularly. Otherwise, you will quickly start to forget key topics.

2 **Retrieval practice makes your memory stronger**
When you recall what you have previously studied, your brain strengthens connections and makes it easier to recall this information in the future.

3 **Spaced practice helps you remember for longer!**
At the end of each topic, we test you, not just on that topic but on previous ones as well. You should regularly return to the Review tasks from previous topics and test your knowledge of 'older material'.

Apply Recall Challenge

1 Know your individuals

How much can you remember from the 'Big Picture' of Elizabethan England? Match each of the key individuals with the correct description.

Individual	Description
The Duke of Norfolk	took part in the slave trade
The Earl of Essex	organised expeditions to North America
Thomas Harman	established a spy network to uncover Catholic plots against Elizabeth
Francis Drake	led a rebellion against Elizabeth in 1601
Walter Raleigh	the Spanish King who planned to invade England in 1588
John Hawkins	a powerful noble involved in a plot to overthrow Elizabeth in 1571
Francis Walsingham	the first Englishman to sail around the world
Mary Queen of Scots	wrote a book warning people about vagabonds
Philip II	Catholic heir to the throne, executed in 1587 for plotting to overthrow Elizabeth

2 Know your key words

Match each key word below with its definition or description.

Key words	Definition
Privy Council	rich and powerful landowners who helped Elizabeth run the country
patronage	homeless people who roamed the country looking for work
nobles	the most important members of the court – a small group of advisers and key ministers who were close to the Queen
the succession	landowners (below the level of the nobles) – many of whom became very wealthy during Elizabeth's reign
the gentry	a system by which Elizabeth could reward loyal nobles and supporters with important positions in the government
vagabonds	priests who arrived secretly in England and aimed to spread the Catholic religion
circumnavigation	a large fleet of ships
excommunication	the question of who would rule the country when Elizabeth died
Catholic missionaries	to travel all the way around the circumference of the world
Armada	a decision by the Pope to expel someone from the Roman Catholic Church

Topic 1 Elizabeth I and her court

1.1 Elizabeth's background and family tree

Focus on ... Elizabeth's childhood

A bright, hard-working student

This portrait of Elizabeth was painted when she was just 13 years old. It gives us clues to Elizabeth's character. The book in the background reflects her love of learning. Elizabeth was a bright, hard-working student. She loved music. She learnt to speak French, Italian, Latin and Greek. Her costume has been carefully painted to show her wealth and status. Our eyes are drawn to the expensive materials used to make her dress and to the fine jewellery.

A difficult childhood

However, the young lady in the picture looks serious and thoughtful. Elizabeth had a difficult childhood. The portrait was probably made by a painter who worked for her father, Henry VIII. He executed her mother, Anne Boleyn, and sent Elizabeth away from the royal **court**.

For many years Elizabeth rarely saw Henry and she lost the title of princess. Despite this, Elizabeth remained proud of him and by the time this portrait was produced, Henry had married for a sixth time and Elizabeth was once again living with her father.

A prisoner in the Tower of London

When Henry died in 1547, Elizabeth's brother Edward became King. But just a few years later Elizabeth's world was turned upside down again when Edward died and her sister, Mary, became Queen.

Edward had been a Protestant, just like Elizabeth, but Mary was a Catholic. She was determined to make England a Catholic country again. Nearly 300 Protestants who refused to change their religious beliefs were burnt at the stake.

When a rebellion broke out in 1554, Mary suspected that her sister was involved. Elizabeth was arrested and charged with **treason**. For two months, Elizabeth was a prisoner in the Tower of London, knowing that if she was found guilty, she would face execution. She survived because not enough evidence was found to prove that she had been involved in the rebellion.

Just four years later Mary died and Elizabeth became Queen.

Reflect

1 Read page 10. You have probably studied Henry VIII before. Link the story of Elizabeth's childhood with what you already know.
   a Why did Henry VIII execute Elizabeth's mother, Anne Boleyn?
   b Why did Henry break away from the Catholic Church and set up the Church of England?
2 Read page 11.
   a Check what you have written down against the details contained in the family tree.
   b What problems did Elizabeth's father, brother and sister face when they ruled England?

Elizabeth's family tree

Henry VIII (ruled 1509–47)

For 40 years Henry was a loyal Catholic but when the Pope refused to give him permission to divorce his first wife, Catherine of Aragon, Henry made himself Head of the new Church of England. Henry closed the monasteries and seized their wealth. As a result, in 1536, a serious rebellion broke out in the north of England. Over 200 rebel leaders were executed.

In 1533, Henry married Anne Boleyn who was already pregnant with Elizabeth. But he had her executed just three years later, accusing her of treason and adultery. Henry's third marriage to Jane Seymour produced a much-wanted son, Edward.

When Henry died, he was short of money because of his expensive wars against France, Scotland and Spain. Around the country the number of people living in poverty was increasing because prices were rising and some people were unemployed.

Married **Catherine of Aragon (divorced)**

Married **Anne Boleyn (beheaded)**

Married **Jane Seymour (died)**

Mary I (ruled 1553–58)

Mary was a devout Roman Catholic and was determined to make England a Catholic country again. She burnt to death more than 300 Protestants who refused to change their beliefs. When she announced plans to marry Philip of Spain many people thought that this would lead to Spain controlling the country. In 1554, a rebellion broke out. Mary thought that Elizabeth had been involved. Mary locked up her half-sister in the Tower of London andexecuted 90 of the rebels.

Mary also faced economic problems. There were two terrible harvests, prices rose sharply and thousands of people died of starvation and disease. Mary made things worse by joining Spain in an unsuccessful war against France. Mary died in 1558, leaving behind enormous debts and an unhappy country.

Elizabeth I

Edward VI (ruled 1547–53)

Edward was only nine years old when he became king. Before his father, Henry, died, he appointed nobles to rule the country for Edward when he ascended the throne. They made the Church of England more Protestant. Decorations, such as wall paintings and stained-glass windows, were removed from churches. A new prayer book, which used English rather than Latin, was introduced. In 1549, Catholics in Devon and Cornwall rebelled because of these changes; 2500 of them were executed for their role in the rebellion.

The number of people living in poverty continued to grow. Harvests were bad so prices rose. Many farm workers lost their jobs when some landowners started enclosing land to keep sheep instead of growing crops. This caused a rebellion in Norfolk in 1549, which resulted in the deaths of 3000 rebels who were killed fighting against soldiers sent by the government to crush the rebellion.

1.2 Court life, patronage and power

Research & Record

How did Elizabeth use the power of patronage and her court?

Read pages 12–13.

1 The diagram below summarises important information that you will need to learn to understand Elizabeth's reign. Read it carefully, then cover it up and try to redraw it **from memory only** using these headings as prompts:
- God
- Monarch
- Nobles
- The gentry
- Everybody else

2 Look again at the diagram in the book. Add any details you have missed and correct any mistakes you made.

3 Write a paragraph explaining why the royal court was important in Elizabethan society.

God

grants power to …

↓

Monarch (Elizabeth I) governs the country

gives rewards and jobs in national government to …

↓

Nobles

Who? The wealthiest landowners

Responsibility? They expected to be the monarch's leading advisers. They were also often appointed as **Lord Lieutenants**. This meant they were responsible for running a whole county and making sure their county could provide well-trained soldiers for the monarch whenever needed.

Loyalty? If the monarch kept them happy they were loyal. But unpopular monarchs could be overthrown by nobles who had their own private army.

give rewards and jobs in local government to …

↓

The gentry

Who? Knights, lawyers and merchants. They owned land but were less wealthy than nobles.

Responsibility? They ran local government as **Justices of the Peace (JPs)**. There were about 40 JPs in each county. They were not paid to do this job, but it gave them a lot of local power and influence. They collected taxes, set wages, kept law and order and decided on punishments for crimes such as assault or burglary.

Loyalty? JPs depended on powerful nobles who recommended them for the role. To keep their job, they had to please the nobles who had helped them gain such an important position.

helped the Queen and the nobles to control …

↓

Everyone else

Who?
- **Yeomen** farmers (who owned their own land)
- Tenant farmers (who rented land from a landowner)
- Craftsmen and craftswomen
- Servants
- Labourers (in the countryside they worked in agriculture, in towns they worked in trades such as textiles)

Responsibility? They worked for the people above them. Men served as soldiers when needed.

Loyalty? They were expected to be loyal to the monarch and obey the local nobles and gentry. However, unpopular religious changes and poor economic conditions could cause rebellions against the monarch or local landowners.

The importance of patronage

People believed their monarch was appointed by God to run the country, so Elizabeth had a lot of power. However, she could not do it all alone! Power, wealth and responsibility passed down through a system known as patronage (as shown in the diagram).

Powerful nobles ran national government for her and the gentry ran local government. However, they always had to ensure they pleased the Queen. If they did not, she could take away their position, wealth or land. That was her real power, not that she made all the decisions herself but because she controlled the people who did.

The importance of the court

The royal court was the centre of government. It was where the Queen brought together the most important people in the country, to give them rewards, settle arguments and ask for advice. However, the court was **not** a place, it was people. It consisted of about 500 nobles, advisers and servants. A **courtier** was anyone who attended the court.

Wherever the Queen went, the court moved with her. The Queen rarely spent more than two weeks in one place. Elizabeth's main palace was at Whitehall, in London, but she regularly stayed at her other palaces, such as Windsor, Greenwich or Richmond. She also visited grand houses belonging to nobles around the country.

Power depended on keeping close to the Queen. The system of patronage meant it was important to keep good relationships with those above you. Ambitious nobles wanted to keep near the Queen so they could win her trust. Every noble wanted a place in Elizabeth's court. If a noble had Elizabeth's favour and patronage they in turn would find it easier to attract loyal supporters from the gentry. This would help to keep their own lands and wealth secure.

The Queen used patronage to keep courtiers loyal. Her favourite courtiers were given accommodation, while others had to find their own place to stay. However, Elizabeth skilfully used patronage to keep as many nobles happy as possible. She shared titles and positions around. Even though she was Protestant, Elizabeth allowed some Catholics to come to court so that she did not lose their loyalty.

Court life

Elizabeth was at the centre of the royal court. She would spend a lot of time in her privy chamber (private rooms). A small group of ladies-in-waiting looked after the Queen. They were usually from wealthy families. Elizabeth expected her ladies-in-waiting to tell her what was happening at court.

Elizabeth used ceremonies and entertainments to demonstrate her power. Courtiers were expected to display their obedience and loyalty towards Elizabeth at ceremonies. Entertainment often involved riding and hunting, as Elizabeth was proud of her abilities in this area. She also loved dancing, music, art and sport. The entertainment was for fun but it was also designed to impress anyone who saw it.

Entertainments at court

- Feasts and banquets
- Dances
- Plays and musical performances
- Jousting tournaments
- Hunting expeditions

1.3 The structure of Elizabeth's government

Research & Record

What was the importance of Elizabeth's Privy Council?

To do well in history you need to be able to support key points with examples. Read pages 14–15 then copy and complete the table. Aim to provide at least two examples to support each statement.

Statement	Supporting examples
The Privy Council provided important **advice** to the Queen.	It advised the Queen on threats from foreign countries.
The Privy Council carried out important **jobs** for Elizabeth.	
Elizabeth **controlled** her Privy Council skilfully.	

The importance of the Privy Council

The most powerful courtiers were members of Elizabeth's Privy Council. They met most days at court. Their job was to advise the Queen and help her run the country. Elizabeth needed the support of as many nobles as possible, but she could only choose a few as her closest advisers. The Privy Council were the people she trusted most.

The **Secretary of State** was the Queen's main adviser and the leading Privy Counsellor.

The role of the Privy Council – remember the 7 Ps

People management

Privy Counsellors organised the work of Justices of the Peace (JPs) and were in charge of various government departments, for example:

- **The Lord Treasurer** was responsible for Elizabeth's finances and spending.
- **The Lord High Admiral** commanded England's Navy, appointed officers and settled disputes at sea.
- **The Lord Chamberlain** ran the royal household, booked Elizabeth's appointments and controlled who could enter the Privy Chamber to see the Queen.

Policy

The Council advised the Queen on important issues such as religion, and foreign policy (for example, when preparing for meetings with foreign ambassadors and dealing with potential threats from other countries).

Pathway to the Queen

The Secretary of State was in most regular contact with the Queen. All letters to the Queen passed through the Secretary of State first.

Propaganda

The Council helped to create a positive image of the Queen through written publications and pictures.

Problem-solving

The Secretary of State was also expected to deal with any day-to-day problems that arose.

Protection

The Council protected the Queen, for example, by using spies to uncover plots against her and helping her crush rebellions. They also organised England's defence against foreign invasion.

Parliament

The Council helped to control what happened in Parliament. They decided what could be debated and made speeches to support or explain the Queen's policies.

How did Elizabeth control her Privy Counsellors?

- **Delay:** She made it clear who would make the big decisions. Elizabeth's counsellors often wanted her to agree quickly to their ideas. However, Elizabeth was a cautious ruler who refused to be rushed into making important decisions. This often frustrated her counsellors but it reminded them who was in control.
- **A small team:** Mary used to have 50 counsellors but Elizabeth limited the team to 19, which made them easier to control. Elizabeth sometimes attended smaller meetings of just eight or nine counsellors.
- **Written records:** Elizabeth used the detailed notes of discussions to question counsellors or catch them out.
- **Careful selection:** Elizabeth chose her counsellors very carefully. She took care not to offend powerful nobles who could turn against her. For example, she did not appoint her closest friend, Robert Dudley, as a counsellor for four years because she thought that might make existing counsellors jealous.
- **Divide and rule:** She deliberately chose counsellors with different viewpoints. This allowed her to listen to all sides then make the final decision herself.
- **Rewards**: If a counsellor did their job well she gave them jobs that allowed them to become rich. This encouraged counsellors to remain loyal to their Queen.
- **Punishments**: If a counsellor upset Elizabeth he would be quickly **dismissed**. Elizabeth also used displays of **anger** at court, often for no apparent reason, to keep counsellors on their toes. Only two counsellors rebelled against her (the Duke of Norfolk and the Earl of Essex). Both were executed.

Apply Exam Practice

Question 2

Explain what was important about Elizabeth's Privy Council. (8 marks)

Use the Exam Tips below to help you.

Exam Tips

Question 2: Developing strong explanations

This type of question is worth 8 marks so you need to do more than simply list reasons why the Privy Council was important. The examiner will look for how well you support **and** develop the points you make.

- You should write two paragraphs – each focusing on a reason why it was important.
- Spend 5 minutes planning your answer then around 10 minutes writing it.

Technique	Advice	Example
Identify a main point you want to make.	Make this your opening sentence.	The Privy Council played an important role in advising the Queen.
Support this point with evidence/examples.	Add examples from the table that you copied from page 14.	For example, they advised her on religion and relations with foreign countries.
Develop this point by explaining why it was important.	This is the part that gets you best marks! Explain why it was important for a ruler to listen to advice.	To make sure she got good advice Elizabeth chose counsellors who had different views on key issues. This helped her to make balanced decisions and to consider different options rather than rushing decisions without thinking through the consequences.

Look at the model above. Use a similar approach to write your second paragraph.

You could focus on the important role counsellors played in helping Elizabeth run the country. Use the examples you have already collected but remember to develop your point by explaining why this was important. Elizabeth skilfully controlled her counsellors but she could not run the country on her own!

1.4 Elizabeth's key ministers

Research & Record

What qualities did Elizabeth look for in her key ministers?

The full Privy Council did not meet every day. A lot of their most important day-to-day business was dealt with by a smaller group of Elizabeth's most trusted counsellors. These were her key ministers. Elizabeth chose them carefully.

As you read the four profiles on pages 16–7 find and record examples of ministers who had each of the key characteristics listed in this bingo card. Can you get a 'full house' of examples?

Characteristics of Elizabeth's key ministers		
Experienced at government	Well educated and intelligent	Different opinions from other counsellors
Willing to disagree with the Queen	Hard-working	Experienced soldier
From the nobility – a powerful family	Well connected (for example, good contacts abroad)	Loyal

Sir William Cecil, Lord Burghley (1520–~~89~~) 98

Background and previous experience

- Member of the gentry
- Studied at Cambridge University
- Well-educated lawyer
- Privy Counsellor for Edward VI

Religion

- A moderate Protestant (did not want to see major changes to the Church)

Personality and relationships with other counsellors

- Intelligent, serious and hard-working
- Wanted to bring the country together and avoid war
- Not afraid to disagree with Elizabeth but very loyal

How he served Elizabeth

- Elizabeth's most trusted adviser; he served her for 40 years
- Became Secretary of State in 1558 (the most important position on the Privy Council)
- Managed meetings of parliament
- Became Lord Treasurer (in charge of government finances) in 1572
- Took over as Secretary of State again in 1590
- Died in 1598. His son, Robert Cecil, took over the position for the rest of Elizabeth's reign.

Sir Christopher Hatton (1540–91)

Background and previous experience

- Member of the gentry
- Studied at Oxford University
- Lawyer

Religion

- Moderate Protestant; sympathised with Catholics

Personality and relationships with other counsellors

- Intelligent, calm and kind

How he served Elizabeth

- Organised the Queen's **progresses** (see page 18)
- Captain of the Queen's bodyguard
- Elected to parliament where he helped Elizabeth control MPs and pass laws
- Made Lord Chancellor in 1587 (in charge of judges and the law courts)
- He died in 1591, leaving behind large debts after building a mansion in Northamptonshire. He refused to sleep in the mansion until Elizabeth had visited.

Sir Francis Walsingham (1532–90)

Background and previous experience

- Member of the gentry
- Studied at Cambridge University
- Well-educated lawyer
- Spoke French and Italian, and had contacts with important people in Europe
- Fled abroad during the reign of Mary I because he did not like her religious policies; returned to the country in 1560

Religion

- A **Puritan** (held extreme Protestant views)
- Wanted to remove decoration from churches and make services simpler
- Believed that Catholics were a threat to the security of the country and that there should be strict laws to control them

Personality and relationships with other counsellors

- A brilliant organiser, secretive and cunning
- Quite a cold character. He never tried to charm or flatter Elizabeth
- Was not afraid to disagree with the Queen. She once threw a slipper at his head when he criticised her. However, he remained loyal to her and Elizabeth valued his clear, honest advice
- Often disagreed with William Cecil

How he served Elizabeth

- Put in charge of Elizabeth's secret service. Controlled a network of spies and informers all over Europe
- Helped uncover a Catholic plot against Elizabeth in 1571
- Took over from William Cecil as Secretary of State in 1572 and served in this position until he died
- In 1586, found evidence that Elizabeth's cousin, Mary Queen of Scots, was involved in a plot to murder her
- It is likely that he died from exhaustion. In 1590, he had a fit but Elizabeth demanded that he return to work. He died just four days later

Robert Dudley, Earl of Leicester (1533–88)

Background and previous experience

- Member of the nobility; youngest son of the Duke of Northumberland
- His father was executed for rebelling against Mary I
- Well educated
- Childhood friends with Elizabeth. Remained close when Elizabeth became Queen. Rumours spread that they were in love
- Fought against France during Mary's reign

Religion

- A Puritan

Personality and relationships with other counsellors

- Very ambitious
- Good organiser
- Disliked William Cecil

How he served Elizabeth

- A loyal adviser to Elizabeth. He was made Earl of Leicester in 1564
- Appointed as Master of the Horse, which made him personally responsible for the Queen's protection
- In 1585, Elizabeth made him an army commander and he was sent to fight Spanish forces in the Netherlands
- In 1588, when the Spanish Armada threated to invade England, he was put in charge of all the land forces guarding the country. He organised Elizabeth's visit to Tilbury, walking beside her as she gave a famous speech to troops guarding London
- His unexpected death in 1588 upset Elizabeth and she kept the last letter he had written to her in a treasure box by her bed for the rest of her life

It is often claimed that the Queen promoted Dudley and Hatton simply because of their good looks and charm. But Elizabeth had other reasons for promoting these two.

- **Dudley came from a powerful family** who the Queen wanted on her side for political reasons.
- **They were excellent courtiers**. They laid on magnificent feasts and entertainments that impressed foreign and English guests.
- **They were intelligent and able**. Before Dudley and Hatton were promoted to the Privy Council, they had already been successful administrators, soldiers or advisers.

1.5 Propaganda and censorship

Research & Record

How did Elizabeth win support and influence people?

1 Elizabeth used propaganda and censorship to influence people. Use pages 18–19 to find at least two more examples of each and add them to a table like this.

2 Study the information about portraits in the box on page 19 then study Sources 1 and 2. Spot three features in each painting that convey these messages. (If you study other portraits online you could find an example of every bullet point.)

Method	Definition	Examples
Propaganda	spreading messages to encourage people to think in a positive way about someone	Showing off Elizabeth's wealth and power through processions and progresses
Censorship	preventing people from saying or publishing things that would damage someone's reputation	

Public image

Elizabeth used her coronation to display her power and wealth. She was carried on a platform covered in golden silk, with her nobles and servants following her. This was followed by ten days of celebration in London and a huge banquet for important nobles and foreign guests.

She used a white 'face mask' to make her look young and to hide the smallpox scars on her face. By the 1590s Elizabeth wore a wig to cover up the fact that she had lost her hair.

Publishing and plays

There were only 60 printing presses in England during Elizabeth's reign. This made it easy for the Privy Council to censor any books or pamphlets that they disproved of. The government briefly shut down London's theatres in 1597 when a play seemed to criticise the Queen.

The Privy Council published their own books to defend decisions that they had taken. They also encouraged others to publish books and plays that showed the Queen in a good light or made fun of enemies such as the King of Spain.

Progresses

Very few people could travel to London to see the Queen, so Elizabeth went on regular tours around the country. These were called progresses. They normally took place during the summer. Elizabeth and her court stayed, free of charge, in houses owned by nobles and the wealthy gentry. The Queen expected them to put on feasts and entertainment for the royal court.

Elizabeth travelled with most of her counsellors, servants and guards. Many nobles spent a huge amount of money trying to impress Elizabeth. The picture on the front of the book shows one of Elizabeth's progresses. It was painted in 1601. Elizabeth is shown with key members of her court.

Portraits

Most of Elizabeth's people never saw her in real life. Their image of the Queen came from her picture on coins or from portraits.

These portraits did not show what Elizabeth actually looked like. They showed a carefully controlled image. They were full of symbols or details that spread positive messages about her (see page 19). Many nobles displayed portraits of the Queen in their houses to show their loyalty. Portraits were also sent abroad to impress foreign rulers.

Artists had to get permission before they could produce a portrait of the Queen. In 1596, any portraits that caused the Queen 'great offence' were burned.

What messages did Elizabeth's portraits put across?

- **That she was England's rightful ruler**. Many Catholics believed that Elizabeth had no right to be Queen. To show that she was a rightful ruler, portraits might include the orb and sceptre (symbols of a monarch's power and authority), the sword of justice, the crown or a Tudor rose.
- **That she was powerful**. Portraits showed her standing on a map of England or with her hand on a globe.
- **That she was wealthy**. Portraits showed her wearing expensive dresses and jewellery.
- **That she was young and healthy**. As Elizabeth grew older, portraits hid any signs of ageing as this was a sign of weakness.
- **That she was a wise and successful ruler.** Sometimes Elizabeth was shown with a serpent (a symbol of wisdom). She was also painted holding a rainbow or bringing in sunshine after a storm, which showed that she was bringing hope to the country.
- **That she protected her people**. Some portraits included symbols to show Elizabeth as the mother of her people, willing to sacrifice herself to protect them.

▲ **SOURCE 1** Elizabeth's coronation portrait, issued by the government in 1559

▲ **SOURCE 2** The 'Pelican' portrait painted in 1574. Elizabeth's brooch shows a pelican. According to legend, the pelican pecked at its own breast so that it could feed its young

Topic 2 The difficulties of a female ruler

2.1 The problems Elizabeth had to face

Focus on ... Thomas Howard, Duke of Norfolk

Power struggles

Thomas Howard, Duke of Norfolk, was wealthy, ambitious and one of the most powerful nobles in England. He was a Protestant but he did not want to see Catholics punished for their beliefs. He was angry when Elizabeth chose William Cecil as her main adviser. He was also jealous about the rise of Elizabeth's favourite, Robert Dudley. Norfolk felt that he was being ignored at court. However, his plan to gain greater influence backfired and helped cause a rebellion in the north of England.

Marriage plans

Norfolk planned to marry Elizabeth's cousin, Mary Queen of Scots. If Elizabeth died without producing any children, Mary had a strong claim to be the next ruler of England. Mary had been brought up a Catholic and had been forced to flee to England after a rebellion led by Scottish nobles. Elizabeth was suspicious of Mary and kept her under guard, well away from the royal court.

Several leading nobles had agreed to Norfolk's plan. Even Elizabeth's favourite, Robert Dudley, was in favour of the plan because he wanted to reduce Cecil's influence at court. However, Dudley soon felt guilty and told Elizabeth about the plan. The Queen was furious and Norfolk went into hiding. When he was captured and put in prison, Norfolk begged Elizabeth to forgive him and told other nobles not to rebel against Elizabeth. However, fearing that they would face prison or even execution because of their involvement in the plan, the Earls of Northumberland and Cumberland organised a large-scale rebellion against Elizabeth in the north of England.

Plots

Norfolk was released from prison but he continued to cause problems for Elizabeth. In 1571, he got involved in the Ridolfi Plot. The plan was to land 6000 Spanish troops in England, where they would join English Catholics who wanted to remove Elizabeth from power. Mary Queen of Scots would be released, she would marry the Duke of Norfolk and become the new Queen of England. The plot was uncovered, and Norfolk was arrested and found guilty of treason. Parliament pushed for him to be executed but Elizabeth was reluctant. Eventually, after changing her mind more than once, Elizabeth signed Norfolk's death warrant. He was beheaded on Tower Hill in June 1572.

Reflect

1. Read about Elizabeth's problems on page 21. Which problems are highlighted in the Duke of Norfolk's story? For example, it highlights political problems as it shows that leading nobles could plot against Elizabeth if they felt excluded from power.
2. Use page 21 to add examples to the PERMS memory aid.

Elizabeth's problems

1 Catholics believed that the Pope was the head of the Church and that churches should be highly decorated. They might rebel if Elizabeth made the Church more Protestant.

2 If Elizabeth did not have children, Mary Queen of Scots had the strongest claim to succeed Elizabeth. But she was a Catholic.

3 King Philip of Spain hoped to marry Elizabeth. But he was a Catholic. If she refused and re-introduced Protestantism, he might attack. Spain was the most powerful country in Europe.

4 Mary I had fought an expensive war against France, so Elizabeth started her reign with massive debts. She did not have enough money to pay for a full-time army.

5 Parliament and the Privy Council wanted Elizabeth to marry and produce an heir. People feared that if she died without an heir there would be a civil war.

6 Parliament was growing more powerful and demanding more say in how the country should be run.

7 Some people feared that a young woman ruler would not have the strength of character needed to control the powerful male nobles.

8 Protestants believed that the monarch should be in charge of the country's Church and that there should be little decoration in churches. Most people in England were Protestants.

9 Puritans were extreme Protestants – they wanted very plain churches and simple services. There were lots of Puritans in parliament.

10 The country's most important industry was making woollen cloth. This was sold abroad but by the early 1550s the trade was collapsing. This meant the government got less money from taxes. Thousands of spinners and weavers were unemployed.

Revision Tip

Create memory aids to help you recall information

A good memory aid is clear, visual and engaging. You have already seen an example on page 6. How does this work?

- An **acronym** can help you remember important facts. In an acronym each letter is the initial of a word you need to remember. In this example, the acronym PERMS helps you remember Elizabeth's main problems.
- When you combine an acronym with a **memorable image** it can give your memory twice as much help. In this example, we have imagined the word PERMS within Elizabeth's hair.

POLITICAL problems – who was in charge
ECONOMIC problems – spending money wisely and not getting into debt
RELIGIOUS problems – whether England should by Protestant or Catholic
MILITARY problems – keeping safe against powerful enemies
SUCCESSION problems – producing an heir

2.2 Relations with parliament

Research & Record

What type of relationship did Elizabeth have with parliament?

Use pages 22–3 to find examples to support the statements in the table. Then copy and complete the table.

Statement	Examples
Elizabeth reacted harshly to criticisms or demands from parliament.	Elizabeth arrested MPs when they put pressure on her to name a successor.
Elizabeth listened to parliament's demands and showed a willingness to compromise.	

Make-up of Elizabeth's parliament

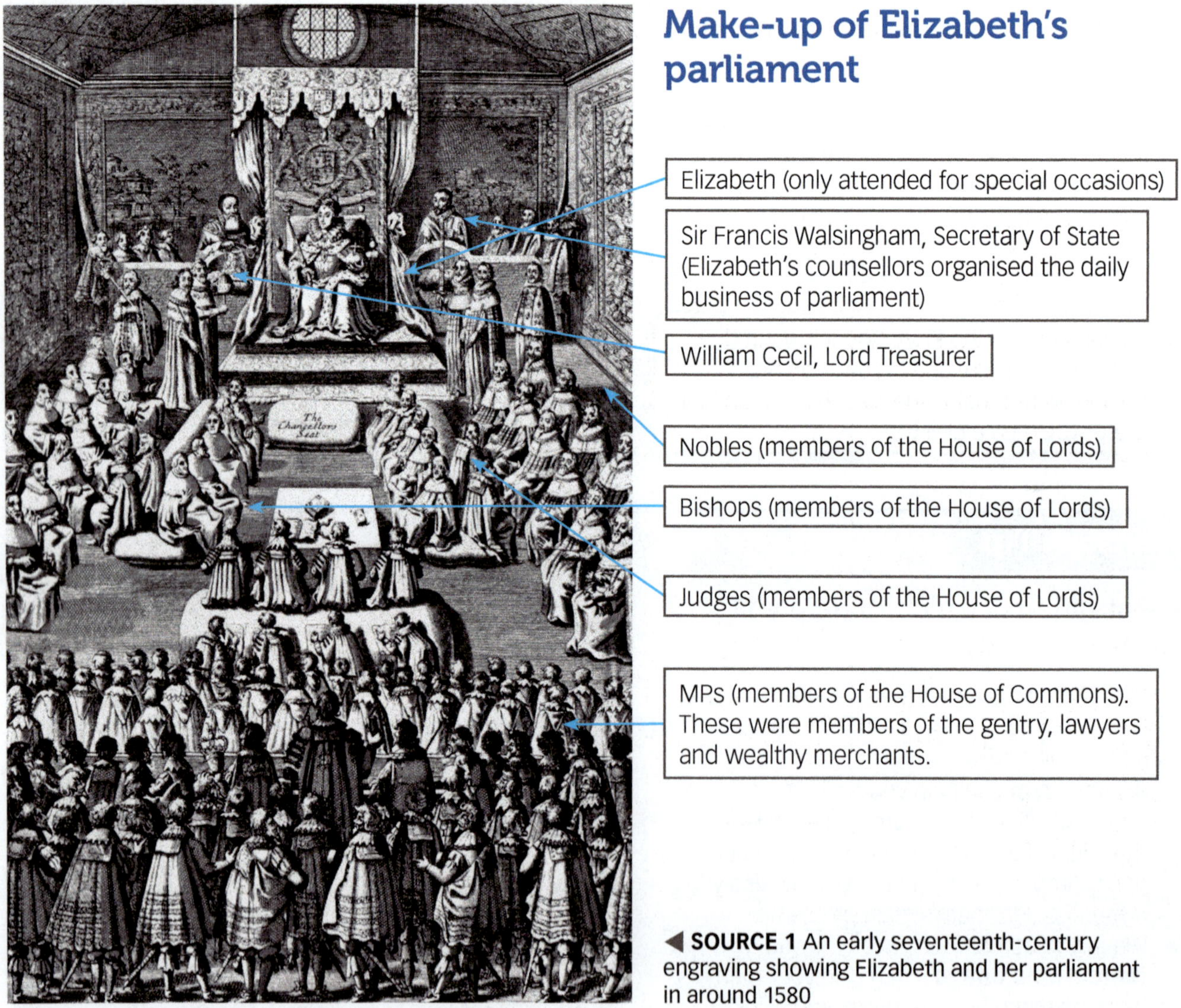

◀ **SOURCE 1** An early seventeenth-century engraving showing Elizabeth and her parliament in around 1580

How Elizabeth controlled parliament

In Tudor times, the monarch decided **when** parliament met. For most of the time Elizabeth could make laws by royal orders without needing any approval by parliament. She had a lot of power. However, if she wanted to raise taxes or make big changes to the law she had to call parliament. Despite her financial problems, parliament only met for a total of 35 months during her 45-year reign. On average, it only met for three weeks each year.

Elizabeth also decided **what** parliament could discuss. She was determined that it should not debate religion or the succession. When an MP called Peter Wentworth put pressure on her to name her successor, Elizabeth had him arrested and imprisoned.

Elizabeth could **dismiss** parliament if it refused to do what she wanted but she was willing to compromise. MPs did get some of the things they wanted, so long as she got the laws and taxes she needed.

Indirectly, through the power of patronage, Elizabeth even influenced **who** could become an MP. Unlike today, MPs were not elected by ordinary people. MPs were proposed by nobles and elected by landowners. The system of **patronage** meant that most nobles wanted to please Elizabeth so they put forward MPs who they knew would support Elizabeth and her government's policies.

Opposition from parliament

Despite her power, Elizabeth did face some opposition from parliament. Some lords who felt sidelined by Elizabeth deliberately put forward MPs who would speak out against her in debates. MPs grew more confident and Elizabeth found it hard to stop them discussing things she did not want them to discuss – such as the succession, marriage and religion.

Example 1: Puritan opposition

Many of Elizabeth's opponents in parliament were Puritans. Their views are summarised below:

- MPs should be allowed to say and discuss what they want in parliament. They should not be arrested or punished if they speak out against the Queen.
- The Queen should change the way the Church is organised. There should be no bishops. Instead, local church groups should have more power and be able to choose their own church leaders. All decoration should be removed from churches.
- The Queen should marry a Protestant prince to make sure that her successor is not a Catholic.

Some Puritans wrote pamphlets criticising Elizabeth when she made decisions they did not approve of. In Elizabeth's opinion they sometimes went too far in speaking out. When John Stubbs (a Puritan MP) wrote a pamphlet criticising her for considering a marriage proposal from a French Catholic he was imprisoned and had his right hand chopped off.

Example 2: Opposition to monopolies

The monarch could grant a **monopoly** meaning someone could be the only person allowed to make or sell a particular product. They faced no competition from other businessmen and could make a lot of money by charging high prices. Towards the end of Elizabeth's reign, many MPs complained about her giving **monopolies** to members of her Privy Council or favourite courtiers. In 1601, Elizabeth compromised and started to cancel some monopolies.

However, these are exceptions. For most of her reign, Elizabeth was able to control parliament and gain the taxes and changes to the law that she wanted.

2.3 The problem of marriage and the succession

Research & Record

Why did Elizabeth never marry?

Read pages 24–5 and copy and complete the table.

Possible husband	Possible advantages of marrying him	Reasons why Elizabeth did not marry him
Philip II	*Spain was a powerful country and could be a good ally.*	
Robert Dudley		
The Duke of Alençon		

The succession problem

When Elizabeth became Queen, everyone expected her to marry quickly. She was the last of Henry VIII's children and if she died without a child the Tudor family line of kings and queens would end. Not knowing who would replace Elizabeth might bring chaos and conflict to the country as different families competed to take over. Elizabeth's Privy Council and her parliaments regularly advised her to marry. They wanted to settle the question of who would replace Elizabeth as soon as possible.

There was no shortage of men who wanted to marry Elizabeth (known as suitors) but she had to balance the advantages of marriage against the potential disadvantages.

Disadvantages of marriage

The suitors

Suitor 1: King Philip II of Spain

Philip II had been married to Mary I and he was keen to regain his title as King of England. Although he was a Catholic, Spain and England had recently been allies in a war against France. However, Elizabeth was fully aware of how unpopular his marriage to Mary had been with the people of England. Their marriage had been a disaster, involving England in an expensive and unsuccessful war against France. As a result, she never seriously considered Philip's marriage proposal. Philip was insulted by Elizabeth's rejection.

Suitor 2: Robert Dudley, Earl of Leicester

During the first few years of her reign there were rumours that Elizabeth was going to marry an English nobleman, Robert Dudley. The couple spent many hours together and had a great deal in common, sharing a love of hunting and dancing. They had been childhood friends.

Elizabeth may well have been in love with him but there was one problem – Dudley was already married. In September 1560, Dudley's wife was mysteriously found dead at the bottom of a set of stairs in their home. An investigation decided that her death was an accident, but many people did not believe it. Elizabeth's close relationship with Dudley had made other nobles jealous and rumours soon started to spread that Dudley had deliberately murdered his wife so that he could marry Elizabeth. Some people even thought that Elizabeth could have been involved. For Elizabeth, this meant that marriage to Dudley was now out of the question as it would risk a big scandal. Dudley waited for years for Elizabeth to change her mind but in 1578 he finally gave up waiting and married her cousin instead.

Suitor 3: Francis, Duke of Anjou and Alençon

Later in Elizabeth's reign, the Duke of Alençon (and later Anjou) seemed to be a serious contender. He was the King of France's younger brother and he regularly visited the Elizabeth's court during the 1570s. Francis was 20 years younger than Elizabeth but, despite the considerable age gap, the pair became very close. The Queen called him her 'frog' and seems to have genuinely enjoyed his company.

This possibility divided opinion in the country. William Cecil was in favour of the marriage. However, France was a Catholic country and Walsingham and Dudley, as well as many Members of Parliament, were firmly against the idea. Opposition to the potential marriage increased significantly after thousands of French protestants were murdered during the St Valentine's Day massacre of 1572. The French became very unpopular in England and many pamphlets were produced against Elizabeth marrying Alençon. In the end, marriage to a French Catholic prince seemed too big a risk and Elizabeth called off the relationship.

The solution to the succession problem

The person who had the strongest claim to succeed Elizabeth was her cousin, Mary Queen of Scots. But Mary had been brought up in France and was a Catholic. After she was executed in 1587 for plotting to kill Elizabeth the succession problem was solved. Mary's only son, James VI of Scotland, now had a strong claim to become King. What's more, he was a Protestant and his claim was recognised by William Cecil. Although Elizabeth refused to officially name James as her heir it became widely accepted that this is what would happen when she died. In 1601, Robert Cecil (William Cecil's son) began to secretly plan with James what would happen when Elizabeth died. In 1603, James became King. England and Scotland now had the same monarch for the first time in history.

2.4 Case study: Kenilworth Castle

Reflect

Why did Robert Dudley spend so much money on Kenilworth Castle?

Read pages 26–7 about the many new features that Dudley added to Kenilworth Castle. Explain why he added these features by linking each one with one of the four motives below:

a To 'show off' his **wealth** and status as an important courtier
b To **entertain** the Queen when she visited
c To **persuade** the Queen to marry him
d To 'show off' how **fashionable** he was

For example:

Dudley spent a lot of money on improving the Great Tower. He wanted to create a large, light room for entertaining the Queen. The hall of the tower was used to display Dudley's finest paintings. His aim was to show off his wealth and how fashionable he was.

A brief history of Kenilworth Castle

- Kenilworth was built in the 1120s as an important royal castle with a Norman keep.
- In the fourteen century the castle was turned into a palace with a comfortable living area and this, combined with the excellent hunting on offer, made it a favourite place for monarchs to stay.
- In 1563, Elizabeth gave the castle to Robert Dudley. A year later she also gave him the title of the Earl of Leicester.

Dudley's improvements

After his wife died, Dudley hoped to marry Elizabeth. He proposed to her at Christmas in 1565. He left court in a sulk when she turned him down.

Elizabeth ordered Dudley to return to court and gave him a lot of money to help him improve Kenilworth. Dudley preserved the original medieval building. However, he also introduced new features reflecting the latest architectural designs of the Elizabethan period (see page 27).

The improvements show Dudley's determination to impress Elizabeth but they also highlight her wish to promote him, as she paid for most of the work.

Elizabeth's visit in 1575

Elizabeth visited Kenilworth in 1575 for 19 days (see picture opposite). This was the longest Elizabeth ever stayed with any member of her court. It became the talk of England.

Nobles were expected to impress the Queen when she stayed with them, but Dudley took things to a whole new level. He put on incredible entertainments. The non-stop programme included hunting, banquets, music and plays. The fireworks he organised could be heard 20 miles away. When Elizabeth complained that she could not see the new garden from her room, his gardeners worked through the night to create a special garden under her window.

The final entertainment should have been a play intended to persuade Elizabeth to marry Dudley but it was delayed due to a rain storm. The Queen rode away, leaving Dudley frustrated.

In 1578, Dudley married Elizabeth's cousin. When Elizabeth found out she was furious, but Dudley was eventually forgiven and the pair remained close until his death in 1588.

Key features and Dudley's improvements

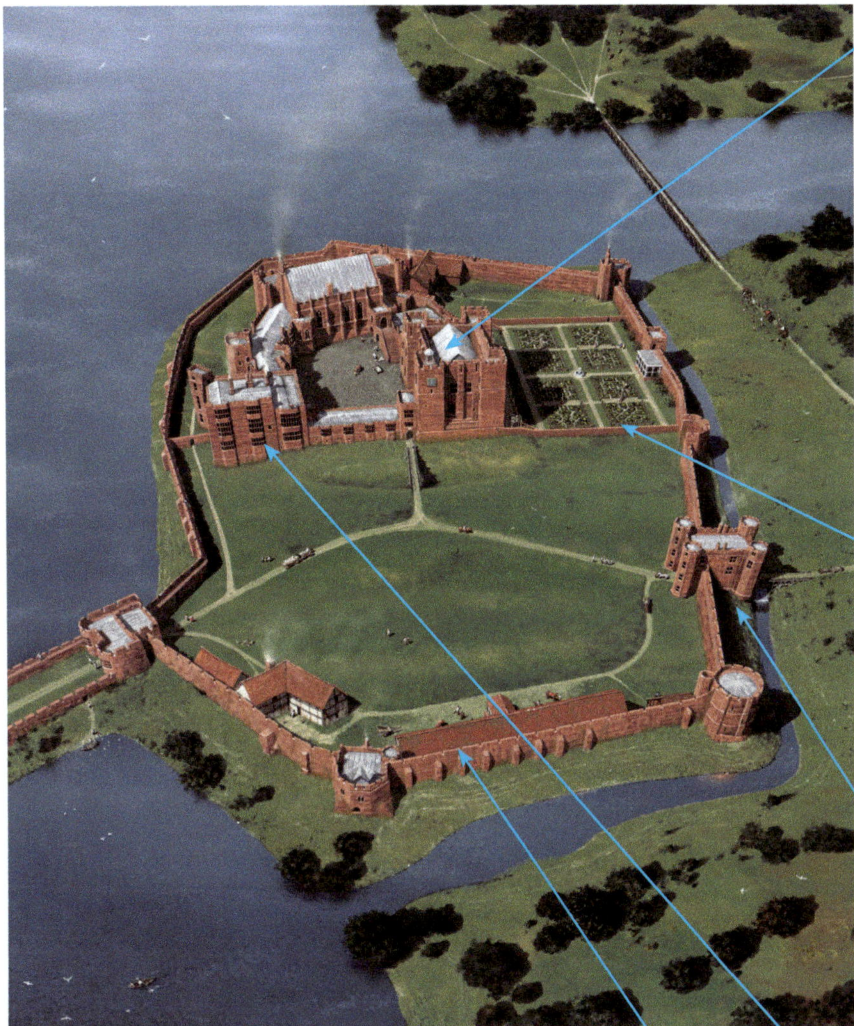

▲ **SOURCE 1** A reconstruction of Kenilworth as it may have appeared in 1575, after Dudley's works

The Great Tower – a large Norman keep which was once the main defensive feature of the castle. Dudley introduced huge windows on the first floor so that light flooded into the enormous room he used for entertaining. The hall of the tower was used to display Dudley's collection of paintings. He had a considerable collection of portraits, including two full length portraits of himself and two of the Queen.

The Privy Garden – created by Dudley for the Queen. The garden was divided into quarters, with an obelisk at the centre of each, surrounded by sweet smelling flowers and trees. At the centre of the garden was a spectacular marble fountain. On the north side was an aviary full of birds.

Leicester's Gatehouse – especially built by Dudley to provide a majestic, grand new entrance to the castle. Guests could reach the enclosed hunting grounds created by Dudley via a 600-foot-long bridge.

Leicester's Building – a four-storey building added by Dudley to provide a place where the Queen could stay on her progresses. She stayed there in 1572 and 1575. The building had massive glass windows with superb views over the grounds of the castle. It was expensively decorated and contained huge fireplaces and had a luxurious room for dancing, a favourite pastime of both the Queen and Dudley.

The stables – filled with the finest horses for Dudley's guests to ride.

Inside the buildings – everything was designed to impress visitors and to show Dudley's status, wealth and fashion sense. There were private rooms for Dudley's family and his guests. Expensive tapestries, imported from the Netherlands, hung from the walls and guests dined using the finest silverware. Linen sheets, feather pillows and curtained four-poster beds were a further sign of wealth.

2.5 Elizabeth's authority at the end of her reign and Essex's rebellion

Research & Record

Title

Use pages 28–9 to fill out a bingo card like this.

Essex's Rebellion, 1603		
3 problems Elizabeth faced at the end of her reign	**3 reasons** why Essex became popular at court	**3 reasons** why Essex rebelled
2 people who plotted against Essex	**2 reasons** why the rebellion failed	**2 key events** that occurred during the rebellion
1 thing the rebellion tells us about rivalry at court	**1 thing** the rebellion tells us about how Elizabeth responded to plots	**1 thing** the rebellion tells us about the problems Elizabeth faced

▲ **SOURCE 1** A portrait of the Earl of Essex painted in c.1595

How did the Earl of Essex become an important figure at court?

1567 Born the son of a leading noble – the Earl of Essex. At this stage he was called Robert Devereux.

1576 – age 9 Became Earl of Essex when his father died

1584 – age 17 Went to the court for the first time. He added glamour to the court. He was young, entertaining and skilled at hunting and jousting. He spent a lot of time with Elizabeth and became one of her favourite courtiers.

1589 – age 22 Went against the Queen's wishes and joined Francis Drake's expedition to Portugal

1590 – age 23 Secretly got married without Elizabeth's permission. She was refused to see him for two weeks.

1593 – age 26 Made a Privy Counsellor

1596 – age 29 Led a successful attack on the Spanish port of Cadiz. He destroyed many Spanish warships and returned to England a national hero.

The position at the end of Elizabeth's reign

Political problems

Throughout her long reign Elizabeth was able to keep the loyalty of her key minsters and leading nobles. However, by 1600, Elizabeth's most trusted and experienced advisers had died. Younger men replaced them who were ambitious, desperate for power and often fought among themselves. In the last years of her reign Elizabeth no longer had such a strong grip on power.

Military problems

England had been at war with Spain for a number of years. Elizabeth spent large sums of money helping rebels fight against Spanish rule in the Netherlands. She also had to send an army to Ireland after a rebellion started there.

Economic problems

Between 1594 and 1597 there were four terrible harvests. Food prices rose and there was widespread hunger. Poverty and crime increased, and there were riots. At the same time, the costs of fighting the war with Spain meant that taxes increased too. This was very unpopular.

Why did the Earl of Essex fall out with Elizabeth?

- Essex wanted to become **Elizabeth's main adviser**, hoping that she would trust him to rule the country as she got older. Instead, while he was away attacking Cadiz, Elizabeth made Robert Cecil (the son of William Cecil) her Secretary of State. Elizabeth also refused to make one of Essex's supporters Lord Deputy of Ireland.
- On his return, **Essex insulted the Queen** and rudely turned his back on her. Elizabeth punched him on the ear. In response, Essex nearly drew his sword and then stormed out of the meeting. Essex was banned from court.
- Elizabeth sent Essex to Ireland to put down a rebellion but when he arrived, he **went against the Queen's wishes** and made peace with the Irish rebels. Elizabeth was furious. She banned Essex from court again and took away his government jobs.
- Elizabeth also **refused to renew his monopoly** for selling sweet wines. Essex was now in debt and his political career lay in ruins.

Essex's rebellion, February 1601

Who?

Essex gathered about 300 supporters including unemployed soldiers, nobles who were either in debt or were disappointed because they had failed to gain influence at court. His plan was to seize the Queen and remove Robert Cecil and his friends from court. He hoped this would force Elizabeth to appoint him and his friends to all the important positions in government.

The trigger

Rumours of Essex's plans spread through London. On 7 February 1601 Essex's supporters put on a performance of Shakespeare's play *Richard II* at the Globe Theatre. It included a scene where the King was overthrown. Elizabeth was furious and ordered Essex to appear before the Privy Council.

The main events – 8 February 1601

- **Essex refused** to appear before the Privy Council, so four Privy Counsellors were sent to his home. Essex arrested them and locked them up.
- He then **marched into the centre of London** with his supporters. Essex hoped that many Londoners would join him, but none did.
- The Privy Council declared that **Essex was a traitor** but promised his supporters that if they left him, they would be pardoned and not punished. Some of his supporters took this offer and surrendered.
- **Essex's position was weakening** so he decided to return home where he intended to use the Privy Counsellors he had locked up as hostages to make a deal with the Queen.
- **The Privy Council sent soldiers** to block Essex's route home. There was some fighting, but Essex made his way to the River Thames and escaped home by boat.
- When he arrived, he found that his **hostages had been released.** Armed soldiers were surrounding his home. Essex had little option but to surrender.
- **His rebellion was over**, just 12 hours after it had begun.

The outcome

Essex was put on trial and found guilty of treason. He was executed at the Tower of London on 25 February.

Part 1: Eliabeth's court and parliament review

Revision Tip: Regularly revisit content to make sure it sticks

You have just completed the first part of the course and it may be tempting to move quickly on to Part 2. However, it is important to build in regular revision activities as you progress through your GCSE course. How do you stop yourself forgetting? The key is to regularly revisit information you have covered. The revision challenges below revisit material from Topics 1 and 2.

Apply Recall Challenges

William Cecil | Robert Dudley
Francis Walsingham | Robert Devereux
Thomas Howard | Christopher Hatton

1 Know your key individuals

a Which of these individuals had the following titles: Duke of Norfolk, Earl of Essex, Lord Burghley?
b Which two rebelled against Elizabeth? When? And why?
c How did the other four help Elizabeth rule the country? What jobs did they do?
d Which individual wanted to marry Elizabeth? Why did she refuse his proposal?

2 Know your key words

Make an A4 copy of this bingo card. You will need plenty of space to write in each box.

Key word		
patronage	propaganda	progresses
monopolies	the succession	Puritans
Lord Lieutenants	Justices of the Peace	Privy Counsellors

a For each key word, write a definition from memory. Then check your definition against the glossary on page 94.
b For each word on the top row, explain how it helped to win Elizabeth support
c For each word on the middle row, explain how it led parliament to criticise Elizabeth
d For each word on the bottom row, explain how it helped Elizabeth govern the country

Summarise

1 Can you remember what this memory aid stands for?

2 The memory aid opposite summarises the importance of the Privy Council to Elizabeth. Write down an explanation and an example for each area.

A = Advice
P = Protection
P = Parliament
L = Law
E = Economic

Apply Exam Practice

These exam-style questions test your understanding of Part 1. Practise them now, then come back to them again later.

Question 1: How convincing?

How convincing is Interpretation A about the relationship that Elizabeth I had with her parliament? Explain your answer using Interpretation A and your contextual knowledge. (8 marks)

▲ **Interpretation A** An engraving of Elizabeth I addressing parliament. This was produced in the nineteenth century

Question 2: Explain

Explain what was important about the system of patronage for Elizabeth and her government. (8 marks)

Question 3: Write an account

Write an account of the ways in which the issue of the succession affected Elizabethan England. (8 marks)

Exam Tips

Question 1: Evaluating interpretations

Step 1: Start by identifying the main message in the interpretation

Focus on the content of the interpretation. Use your inference skills to think carefully about what is being suggested. For example:

- Look at Elizabeth's expression and body language in the image. Does she look calm and in control of parliament?
- How are people around her reacting? Do they look supportive and respectful?

Step 2: Use your own knowledge of this topic to evaluate this message

- In one paragraph you could make the point that at times Elizabeth faced opposition from her parliaments and MPs were not always respectful! This angered her.
- In your second paragraph you could make the point that for most of the period Elizabeth was in control of parliament and managed it effectively.
- Make sure you give examples to support the points you make in each paragraph.

Step 3: Reach a judgement

- Make a clear overall judgement on the extent to which the message given in the interpretation is convincing. Is it very convincing or only partly convincing?

Question 2: Explain

Use the Exam Tips on page 15 to help you. Remember to:

- plan your answer using two paragraphs
- start each paragraph with a main point
- then support and develop it.

For this question your two paragraphs could explain how:

- the system of patronage helped Elizabeth keep her leading nobles happy **and**
- it helped her run the country. Remember that the people she gave positions of power to then passed some of this power on to other groups in the hierarchy (see page 12).

Question 3: Write an account

Read the question carefully. It is **not** asking for a description of who wanted to marry Elizabeth. The focus is on how uncertainty over Elizabeth's succession affected the country. Plan two paragraphs:

- The first could focus on how the uncertainty led to criticism from parliament and fears of a civil war between rival families, or Catholic, Mary Queen of Scots taking over.
- The second could look at how the issue developed – how Elizabeth responded and how not marrying had some advantages for her.

Topic 3 A 'Golden Age'

3.1 The structure of society, living standards and fashions

Focus on ... Bess of Hardwick

From modest beginnings ...

This portrait is of Bess of Hardwick and by the time it was painted she had risen to be one of the wealthiest people in Elizabethan England. The expensive black velvet dress and the five ropes of pearls stretching from her neck all the way down to her waist show off her tremendous wealth and status. Bess had not been born into a wealthy family. Her father was a member of the Derbyshire gentry who owned a small manor house. When he died, he left each of his daughters a small sum of money.

... to great riches

Bess married four times and each of her marriages made her richer and more powerful. By the age of 15 Bess was married to Robert Barlow but he died a few months after the wedding. Her second husband was Sir William Cavendish. He worked for the government at the time that Henry VIII closed the monasteries. Cavendish became very rich from buying monastery land and renting it out.

When Cavendish died, Bess married one of Elizabeth's favourite nobles, Sir William St Loes. This gave Bess access to the royal court and she became a lady of the Queen's privy chamber. When William died, Bess inherited a large amount of his land.

Her last marriage was to George Talbot, Earl of Shrewsbury. He was head of one of the oldest and richest families in England. He owned vast amounts of farmland, plus coal mines, glassworks, iron foundries and ships. The Earl died in 1590 leaving Bess, in her early 60s, one of the richest people in England.

Hardwick Hall

Bess of Hardwick's story reflects how for some people, Elizabeth's reign saw growing prosperity. The gentry were better off than ever before, and they showed off their wealth by building impressive houses with fashionable furnishings.

During the 1590s Bess built Hardwick Hall, the magnificent house you can see on pages 36–7. It took about seven years to complete. Bess lived there until she died in 1608. Hardwick Hall was built to impress. It was a way for Bess to show how wealthy she was and her status in society.

Reflect

1. Read page 32. What made Bess' last three husbands rich and powerful?
2. Look at the diagram on page 33. Some of this information should already be familiar to you from page 12. Bess of Hardwick was born into the gentry. Can you remember what role in governing the country was played by the:
   - gentry?
   - nobility?

   You can check to see if you were right by turning back to page 12.
3. Look forward to the picture of Hardwick Hall on pages 36–7. What new architectural features stand out?

Elizabethan society – a hierarchy

Society in Elizabethan times was very structured. As the diagram below shows, there was a clear **hierarchy** – with the monarch at the top and the labourers and poor at the bottom.

The Queen
Her wealth came from her land. She made all the important decisions but was advised by leading nobles.

The nobility (Dukes, Earls and Lords)
About 50 families. They owned huge areas of land that made them wealthy and powerful. A leading nobleman might own tens of thousands of acres in different estates (areas of land) across England.

The gentry
About 10,000 families. Most gentry owned an estate of a few hundred acres. They might also be knights or lawyers. During Elizabeth's reign some members of the gentry (like Bess of Hardwick) became very wealthy.

Merchants
About 30,000 families. They lived in towns and could become wealthy through trade. Like the gentry, merchants were growing in power and influence during Elizabeth's reign.

Yeomen and tenant farmers
About 100,000 families. Yeomen owned their own land (often more than 50 acres) and tenant farmers rented land. Both employed farm labourers.

Craftspeople, labourers and servants
About 500,000 families (approximately half the population). In towns, they worked in trades such as textiles and leather. In the countryside, they mainly worked on farms.

Improving living standards ... for some!

Living standards and conditions improved for the gentry, merchants and many yeomen.

- **Chimneys.** These made a massive difference. Smoke no longer needed to escape through the thatched roof so rooms could have proper ceilings and houses could be divided into upstairs and downstairs rooms.
- **Glass windows**. These replaced small windows, covered with wooden shutters. This improvement meant that the inside of homes could now be lighter and warmer.
- **Diet**. Yeomen and their families usually ate well, although they could not afford the fine wines and huge feasts that the gentry enjoyed.

However, for those at the bottom of the social hierarchy, life could be very different.

- **Poverty**. Many craftspeople, labourers or servants were forced into poverty by bad harvests, rising prices and unemployment. Farmers only employed labourers when they needed them, at busy times of the year such as harvest. Most labourers had to go from farm to farm looking for work. They struggled to pay their rent and buy food for their families.
- **Bad housing**. Labourers' cottages were small, with no upper rooms, no chimneys, no glass windows and a bare earth floor. They were unhealthy. Harmful smoke from the fire filled the room as the only way it could escape was through the thatched roof. The small shuttered windows made it dark inside.

3.2 Growing prosperity and the rise of the gentry

Research & Record

How did the gentry get rich and how did they use their wealth?

1 Read the diagram below which shows why the gentry grew increasingly wealthy. How many of these reasons did you find in Bess of Hardwick's story on page 32?

2 Read about how the gentry expressed their wealth and status on page 35. How did Elizabethan England change as a result of a rise in the prosperity of the gentry? Copy and complete the table below, making sure you explain why the change happened.

Change identified	Explanation
More young people going to university	The gentry hoped that this would help their children gain a career at court

How did the gentry grow richer and more powerful in Elizabethan England?

Getting rich in Elizabethan England

Patronage
Some members of the gentry were given an important job in the government. Like her father Henry, Elizabeth sidelined any noble she viewed as a threat. She preferred to give jobs to talented members of the gentry such as Robert Cecil.

Marriage
Marrying into a richer family was one way of acquiring wealth.

Politics
The gentry dominated the House of Commons (as MPs) and helped to run local government as Justices of the Peace. This gave them political power and influence.

Voyages of exploration and colonisation
Some members of the gentry invested in overseas voyages. Sir Francis Drake made a lot of money for those who invested in his expeditions.

Monasteries
After Henry VIII closed the monasteries, more land was available than ever before. The monasteries had owned about a quarter of the land in England. The gentry bought monastery land and rented it out to farmers.

Rising prices
Rising food prices were bad for the poor but they helped farmers make bigger profits.

Industry
Some found they could make more money from their land by rearing sheep to supply the cloth industry, or by mining coal or making iron.

How did the gentry express their wealth and status?

As the gentry became richer, they were keen to impress others in society and gain greater influence.

1 **Education**

The number of children going to school increased during the Elizabethan period. A university education was increasingly seen as essential if you wanted a career at court. People were keen to show off how well educated they were, displaying their books in libraries in their homes.

2 **Entertainment and feasting**

Wealth gave the gentry plenty of opportunities to enjoy themselves when they were not working. They held banquets, and went hunting and to the theatre.

An Elizabethan feast could last for more than two hours. A range of meats and fish were often served. In country houses, servants would carry the food from a kitchen on the lower floor to the great chamber, where guests would drink fine wines imported from France and Italy.

3 **Fashion**

Fashion became a status symbol. Fine clothes and even make-up showed your position in society. Women used make-up to whiten their face because not having a tanned face was a sign that they did not have to work outside! Clothes became so significant that laws were passed to control what people wore. They could only wear clothes that reflected their place in the social hierarchy.

4 **Country houses**

The gentry built themselves magnificent new houses using brick or stone, with large glass windows. They included the latest architectural fashion and styles to show their wealth and status. Inside, country houses were far more comfortable and richly decorated than before. They had impressive fireplaces, large libraries and the walls were covered with expensive paintings and tapestries.

- **Bess of Hardwick** employed the famous architect, Robert Smythson, to make sure her new home would amaze everyone who saw it. Architects such as Smythson were heavily influenced by Italian Renaissance-style architecture. Smythson focused on symmetry and size. He used expensive glass and built decorative, tall chimneys.
- Another member of the gentry who rose to the top was **William Cecil**. Due to his role as Elizabeth's key minister and most trusted adviser, Cecil grew very wealthy. He was given the title Lord Burghley in 1571 and built **Burghley House** in Lincolnshire (see Source 1). As you can see from the photograph, it was built to impress. Houses such as Burghley and Hardwick Hall deliberately matched the splendour and size of those owned by the nobility.

▲ **SOURCE 1** Burghley House

3.3 Case study: Hardwick Hall

Reflect

What do Elizabethan country houses tell us about Elizabethan society?

1 What similarities can you see between Hardwick Hall and other country houses such as Burghley? Look for at least three.

2 What does Hardwick Hall tell us about Elizabethan England? Structure your answer using these headings:

- Architectural styles
- Fashion
- Living standards for the gentry
- The structure of society

What motives did Bess have for building Hardwick Hall?

- **Ambition** – Bess wanted a house fit for royalty. She hoped that a member of her family would marry into the royal family.
- **To impress the royal court** – Bess was good friends with Elizabeth and key members of the Tudor court (such as William Cecil and Sir Francis Walsingham).
- **To impress visitors** – Bess was sending out a social message. Hardwick Hall was a status symbol that showed wealth, power and prestige.
- To show her **loyalty** to the Queen.
- To show how **educated and fashionable** she was.

▲ 1

Inside Hardwick Hall

Decoration and furnishing were used to show how rich and fashionable Bess was.

- She owned a large collection of tapestries. Those using silk or metal thread were most expensive and so were displayed in the rooms of highest status (see picture 2).
- Bess had French furniture which showed how fashionable she was.
- Bess also had one of the largest collections of Turkish carpets in the country.

▲ 2

Key features of Hardwick Hall

1 Members of the gentry wanted large well-kept **gardens** close to their homes

2 **The Great Chamber** – used for receiving important guests and holding banquets (see picture 2 on page 36)

3 Elegant **staircases** lead to the great chamber

4 **The Long Gallery** – 162 feet long and used for indoor exercise, dancing and conversation (see picture 1 on page 36)

5 The west side **loggia** can be seen on the ground floor. These were becoming fashionable

6 **Glass** was a status symbol and the greatly increased height of the windows at Hardwick made them all the more impressive

7 The layout models the **hierarchy** of Elizabethan society. The ceilings and windows increase in height from bottom to top.
- Servants were on the ground floor
- Bess used the first floor

8 Potential royal visitors would stay in **bedchambers** on the second floor

3.4 Elizabethan London

Signs of increasing prosperity could also be seen in Elizabethan towns. This was especially true in London. It was the capital city and by far the most important place in England. London's population grew from just over 50,000 in 1520, to an estimated 200,000 in 1600. The picture below gives us an idea of what London looked like at the time and some clues as to why London became so important.

Research & Record

What made London such an important city?

Read pages 38–9.

1 Explain why London became so important during the Elizabethan period. Aim to write three paragraphs. The first should cover political reasons, the second economic reasons and the third cultural reasons.
2 What were the negative consequences of the growth in London's population?

The centre of power

On the north bank of the river we can see Whitehall Palace. This was where Elizabeth stayed most often. We have already seen how the royal court was the centre of government and the place to be for those who wanted patronage from the Queen. This meant that ambitious nobles, the gentry and merchants flocked to London hoping to be rewarded with important positions. Wealthy individuals bought fine houses near the river. Along the Strand (just before St Paul's Cathedral) you can spot Essex House and Burghley House, the London homes of the Earl of Essex and William Cecil.

Others moved into London to be near the law courts and parliament. There was an increase in the number of lawyers living in London.

The centre of entertainment

On the south bank of the river the large church in the foreground was called St Mary Overie (now Southwark Cathedral).

You can also see three theatres: the Bear Garden, the Swan and the Globe. The Bear Garden or Bear Pit was used for 'animal sports' such as bear-baiting and bull-baiting. The size of the Swan and the Globe reflect the growing popularity of the theatre. At the start of the Elizabethan period there were no theatres in London but by 1600 thousands of Londoners, rich and poor, attended the theatre regularly.

The centre of trade

On the right-hand side of the picture you can see St Katharine Docks. In the Elizabethan period, trade expanded with other countries. London became England's most important port. In the 1590s, 93 per cent of cloth exports went through London. Merchants lived off the profits from trade. In towns with a thriving port, such as London, they were able to build up large fortunes and their wealth rivalled that of the gentry. Some merchants became mayors and gained political influence.

Unemployed people from the countryside also came to London as there were opportunities to earn money as sailors, builders or dress makers. Small business owners (such as shoemakers and bakers) did well as an increasing population meant greater demand for their goods. The arrival of wealthy members of the nobility and the gentry into London was particularly good news for those involved in the food and clothing trades.

Comparing London to other towns

There were opportunities for individuals in other towns to become wealthy – for example as merchants, lawyers or those involved in the metal industries. There were also apprenticeships for skilled labourers.

No other city could compare with London's size or importance, however. The next largest city, Norwich, had a population of just 12,000. Smaller ports in England lost trade to London. Merchants in London were far wealthier than those in other towns. Ambitious merchants would move to London where there was a greater chance to gain financial backing and make profits.

And in all towns, London included, the poor faced food shortages and overcrowded housing. There were more opportunities than in the country but many unskilled labourers who came to London still struggled to pay their rent and feed their families.

▲ **SOURCE 1** The engraving shows a view of London in around 1600. It was produced by Claes Visscher and was first published in 1616. London Bridge dominates the right-hand side of the picture. The area south of the Thames could be accessed by London Bridge which was covered with shops and houses. London's growth created problems. The growth of the docks around London Bridge led to overcrowding and poor conditions in that area. This increased the risk of disease. In 1571, London was described as 'a stinky city, the filthiest of the world'. Horses excreted urine and dung, which clogged the streets. Pigs and dogs roamed free, while on market days, cattle and sheep dropped their dung as they were driven through the streets to the markets. There were only a few public lavatories and waste was often thrown into the river, which was also the main source of drinking water

3.5 The Elizabethan theatre and its achievements

Research & Record

Why did the theatre become so important in Elizabethan England?

Read pages 40–1.

1 Organise the cause cards on page 41 under the following headings:
   - **Political** reasons why the theatre became popular
   - **Economic** reasons why the theatre became popular

2 Use the cause cards to write two paragraphs explaining why the theatre became an important feature of Elizabethan London.

Why were the first theatres established in London?

There wasn't a single theatre in England when Elizabeth became Queen. There were bands of actors who travelled from town to town, but local councils thought that they were a threat to law and order and should be punished as vagabonds (beggars).

However, in London, some powerful nobles, such as the Earl of Leicester (Robert Dudley) and Sir Francis Walsingham, protected groups of actors and gave them financial support. These powerful nobles made sure that members of theatre companies were not treated as vagabonds.

To start with, the acting companies performed wherever they could. The first purpose-built theatre was then built in 1576 (see map). Many more followed and going to the theatre became a very popular pastime. By 1600, many Londoners were going to the theatre at least once a week.

It was a remarkable change. At the start of Elizabeth's reign, playwrights and actors were looked down upon. By the end, theatre owners, actors and writers were becoming famous, respected and wealthy.

Where were the main theatres built?

In 1576, James Burbage built the first large, purpose-built theatre (which he called The Theatre) just outside London, in Shoreditch. Burbage asked for the Earl of Leicester's protection and patronage. The Queen granted a licence to the Earl for a theatre company to perform there which would bear his name – the Earl of Leicester's Men. Burbage's theatre was a great success. Other people saw the chance to make money and soon other theatres, such as The Curtain were built nearby.

Theatres were usually built outside the city walls as the area inside was controlled by the city authorities. The authorities were worried about the large, noisy crowds that gathered at the theatre. As a result, towards the end of Elizabeth's reign, theatres such as the Globe, the Rose and the Swan were built in Southwark, south of the River Thames.

▼ Theatres in London

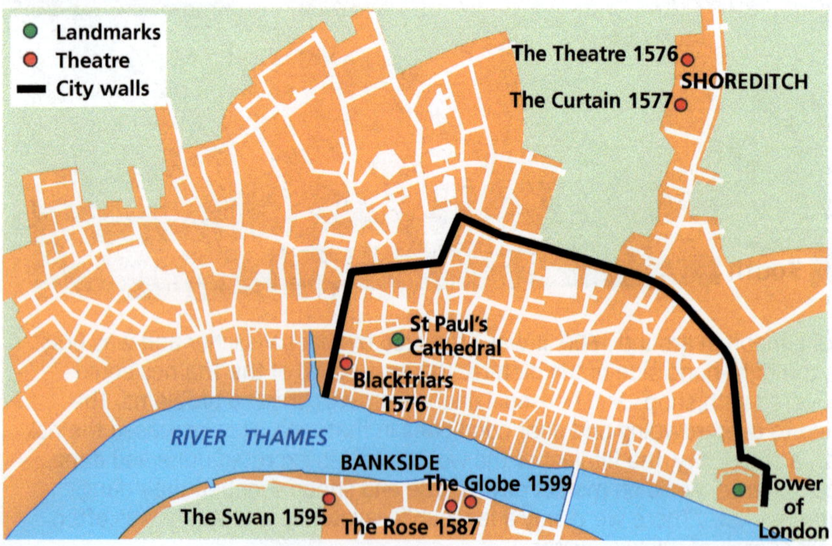

Why did the theatre become popular?

Cause cards

1 Clever playwrights

The plays were entertaining. The themes were relevant to the audience. Theatres were expected to put on a new play every couple of days, so there was a great variety of plays that appealed to everyone's tastes. This meant that many people wanted to watch them.

Theatres become more professional and audiences liked the clever and dramatic stories, written by playwrights such as William Shakespeare and Christopher Marlowe. People loved Shakespeare's comedies and plays about history.

2 Court patronage

Members of the royal court, like Robert Dudley, hoped that people who attended the plays put on by his company (the Earl of Leicester's Men) would be impressed and thank him for putting on the plays they enjoyed. They also knew that Elizabeth loved watching plays, so supporting a theatre company was a way of becoming popular and gaining the approval of the Queen. Other members of the royal court tried to match Dudley by setting up their own companies.

- Lord Hunsdon, the Queen's cousin, set up the Lord Chamberlain's Men, of which William Shakespeare was a leading member.
- Their main rivals were the Admiral's Men, set up by Lord Howard after he became England's Lord High Admiral.

3 The approval of the Queen and her government

Elizabeth loved the theatre and this changed the attitudes of local councils who had previously banned plays in their towns. Her attitude also made ambitious courtiers keen to provide patronage and support for theatre companies. The Queen never attended performances in the London theatres. Instead, new plays were often performed for her at the royal court before they went 'public'.

Instead of seeing the theatre as a threat, Elizabeth's advisers started to see its potential for propaganda (spreading positive messages about Elizabeth and her family) and keeping order in society.

Shakespeare's plays often contained messages that Elizabeth's government approved of. They showed:

- the importance of order and keeping the **social hierarchy** in place (The Elizabethans believed everyone and everything had its own place in the social hierarchy – see page 33.)
- the triumph of good over evil
- Elizabeth's family (the Tudors) in a good light. For example, Shakespeare's play ***Richard III***, presented Elizabeth's grandfather, the first Tudor king, Henry VII, as the saviour of the nation. His enemy, Richard III (whom Henry VII killed in order to take his throne), is shown as a hunchbacked, evil monster who murdered his nephews and many others.

4 A distraction for the poor

By the end of Elizabeth's reign, London was a busy city but not everyone was getting richer. Many members of the lower classes were living in poverty. Elizabeth's government believed that theatre entertainment could act as a distraction for the large number of poor people and discontented lower classes, making a rebellion less likely.

5 Wealth

London's population was increasing quickly, and many people were getting wealthier. The theatre was popular with all sections of society. Wealthy traders and manufacturers who lived in London, and their workers, had the money to watch plays. Theatres were making a lot of money by the 1580s. People were willing to invest their money in building theatres because they saw that profits could be made.

3.6 Attitudes to the theatre

Research & Record

Why did people have different attitudes towards the theatre?

1 Read page 42. What reasons did people have for visiting the theatre? Find and record evidence to support the statements in the table. Then copy and complete the table.

2 Read page 43. Explain why some people opposed the theatre. Aim to write two paragraphs:
- In the first paragraph explain why some people thought the theatre was 'dangerous'.
- In the second paragraph explain why some people thought the theatre was 'disrespectful'.

Statement	Supporting evidence
It was a social occasion.	Lots of people went to the theatre so it was a great place to meet people.
The theatre was entertaining and dramatic.	
It was near other forms of entertainment.	

What was it like to visit an Elizabethan theatre?

The painting below shows the Rose Theatre on the south bank of the River Thames. People are arriving by boat.

- A visit to the theatre was not just about watching a play. It was also an afternoon out, a chance to meet other people. **Before the play** they might first visit a riverside inn. They could also see bear-baiting at the Bear Garden nearby.

▲ **SOURCE 1** A recent painting of the Rose Theatre by the artist Peter Jackson

- There was no artificial lighting, so plays were **performed in daylight** – usually starting at 3 p.m. The start was announced by **blowing a trumpet**.
- **Coloured flags** flew above the theatre to show the type of play: white for comedy, red for history, black for tragedy.
- **People from all social classes** went to the theatre. The Rose Theatre could accommodate over 2000 spectators. Entrance fees were affordable even for the poor.
- There was no scenery but actors wore **colourful costumes**. Acting was not considered a suitable job for women, so young boys took the female roles.
- The audience wandered around during performances, eating and drinking. **It was rowdy**. They responded to the play by clapping, booing and even throwing things at the actors.
- **After the play** some people visited gambling dens, brothels and beer houses before going home.

Why was there opposition to the theatre?

1 **Fear of disease**
By the 1590s, an estimated 15,000 people visited the London theatres each week. People believed that with such large crowds of people gathered together, diseases would spread. All theatres were closed in 1593 because of the fear that the large crowds would help spread the bubonic **plague**.

2 **Fear of crime**
The City of London authorities did not want theatres built within the city walls because the theatres had a poor reputation and were thought to encourage crime and disorder. In 1574, the Council of London banned plays within the city limits and by the 1590s all theatres had moved south of the River Thames.

3 **Fear of plots or rebellions**
The government was worried that large crowds of poor people could riot or join together to rebel against the government. The fact that the Earl of Essex attended a performance of *Richard II* (a play about a monarch being overthrown) at the Globe the night before his unsuccessful rebellion increased fears that plays could spark rebellions.

4 **Religious beliefs**
Puritans believed that theatres were the work of the devil. Puritans and other religious figures criticised the theatre for distracting people from religion.

How did Puritan opposition help to build the Globe?

James Burbage built his first theatre just outside London's northern city wall. He owned the building, but it was on land belonging to a Puritan called Giles Allen. When Burbage's lease ran out, Allen refused to renew it. So, Burbage and his actors, helped by some labourers, dismantled The Theatre while Allen was away at his country house for Christmas.

During the spring and summer of 1599, they then used the timbers to build a new, larger theatre on the south bank of the Thames. They called it the Globe. The Globe's story continues on the next page.

Summarise

Add your own examples and key points to this memory aid in order to show the main reasons why:

- The theatre became popular
- There was opposition to the theatre.

e.g. ...

By 1600 London's population had grown to 200,000

Many people had more money to spend on entertainment

e.g. ...

e.g. Shakespeare's plays ...

1593: Theatres closed because of the plague

e.g. Giles Allen ...

e.g. ...

3.7 Case study: The Globe

Reflect

What can the Globe tell us about Elizabethan England?

Read page 44 and use the knowledge you have built up about Elizabethan theatres from the last pages 40–43 to make notes and discuss what the Globe can tell us about the following features of Elizabethan England:

1. **Politics** (patronage, propaganda and place in the social hierarchy)
2. **Economics** (growing prosperity and population growth)
3. **Religion** (reasons for opposition to the theatre)
4. **Culture** and leisure (how people spent their free time)

Then use these notes to answer the Practice Exam Question opposite.

Apply Exam Practice

Question 4: Evaluate

Use the notes you have just made and the Exam Tips on page 45 to answer this question.

'The main change that Elizabethan theatres demonstrated was the growing prosperity of people living in London.' How far does a study of the Globe support this statement?

(16 marks)

Features of the Globe Theatre

The Globe could hold almost 3000 spectators. The money to build the new theatre came from two of James Burbage's sons (Richard and Cuthbert), William Shakespeare and actors from the Lord Chamberlain's Men theatre company. It was almost circular and three storeys high. The picture below is based on architectural evidence. The original Globe burnt down in 1613.

The audience

The most expensive seats above the stage were called the **Lord's Rooms**. They had cushions and were visible to the rest of the audience. This was the place to be seen!

The covered **galleries** were mainly for the gentry. Tickets cost 2–3 pennies. The thatched roof protected you from bad weather.

The **pit** was where poorer people stood to watch the plays. You would get wet if it rained but it was cheap at a penny a ticket.

The actors

The **stage** included trapdoors and had a wall at the back, which was where actors made their entrances and exits.

The **hut** was above the stage and provided storage space and an area for special effects.

Behind the stage was the **tiring house**, where the actors put on their costumes and collected their props.

Exam Tips

Question 4: Evaluate

Think before you write using the **'4Ds'**

Decode *the question: work out the focus of the question.*

Staying relevant to the question is crucial. Including information that is not relevant or writing about the wrong topic wastes time and gains no marks. Here's how to decode a question.

What is the conceptual focus?
The historical concept is change. The statement identifies an important economic change (growing prosperity). Think carefully about how the Globe reflects other changes in society – for example political, cultural or religious changes.

What is the content focus?
The focus is on the Globe Theatre, but you can use your wider contextual knowledge of how the growth of theatres reflected major changes in Elizabethan society.

'The main change that Elizabethan theatres demonstrated was the growing prosperity of people living in London.' How far does a study of the Globe support this statement? (16 marks)

What are the command words?
The question is asking you to evaluate how far a study of the Globe supports a statement. The Globe did demonstrate a key change in Elizabethan society – that people had become more wealthy and prosperous, spending their money on going to and financially supporting the theatre. But is this the main change demonstrated by the Globe?

How many marks are available?
16 marks indicates that you should spend about 20 minutes answering this question. Aim to write four paragraphs using the advice provided on planning below.

Decide *how to organise your answer before you start to write.*

You should aim to weigh the importance of the change stated in the question against **two other** important changes. Use your first paragraph to explain and evaluate the importance of the change stated in the question. Then add two more paragraphs explaining how other changes in society led to the growth in theatres such as the Globe. End with a concluding paragraph in which you reach a clear, explained judgement on how far a study of the Globe supports the statement in the question.

Develop *your answer – make sure you explain and support the points you make.*

Do not simply say that the growing prosperity of people in London led to theatres such as the Globe being built – prove it. Explain how the Globe was built because the men who paid for it knew that people had more money to spend on entertainment. If it had not been a time of prosperity, people would not have been able to afford to go to the theatre.

Demonstrate *complex thinking.*

Complex thinking earns top marks in the exam.

Look for links between changes (or causes if this is the focus of the question).

For example, without political changes, such as the patronage of important courtiers, actors and playwrights might not have felt safe to set up theatre companies, no matter how much money they could earn. Remember that the company that owned and performed at the Globe had the patronage of the Lord Chamberlain who was an important member of Elizabeth's Privy Council.

Topic 4 The poor

4.1 Attitudes towards poverty

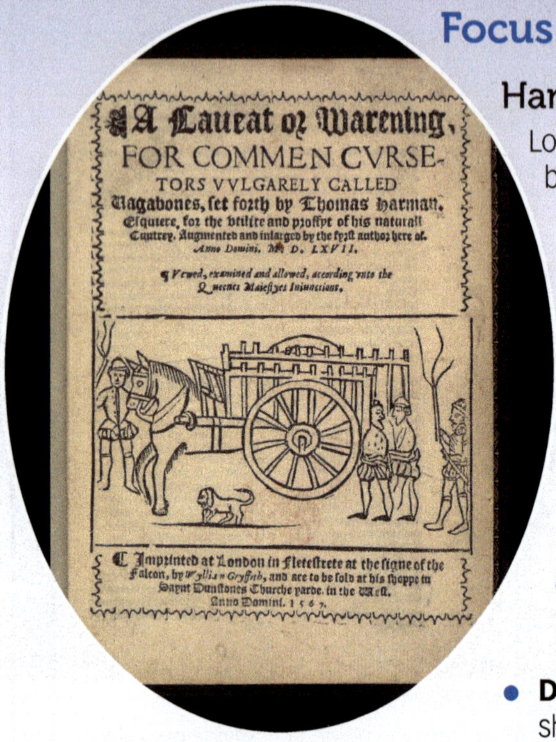
A Caueat or Warening, FOR COMMEN CVRSETORS VVLGARELY CALLED Uagabones, set forth by Thomas Harman, Esquiere, for the vtilitie and proffyt of his naturall Countrey. Augmented and inlarged by the fyrst author here of. Anno Domini. M. D. LXVII.

Vewed, examined and allowed, according vnto the Queenes Maiesties Iniunctions.

Imprinted at London in Fleetstrete at the signe of the Falcon, by Wylliam Gryffith, and are to be sold at his shoppe in Saynt Dunstones Churche yarde. in the West. Anno Domini. 1567.

Focus on ... Thomas Harman

Harman's warning

Look closely at this book cover. It uses an Elizabethan font but can you work out what it says?

In this famous book, which was written to entertain as much as inform, Thomas Harman warned people about the alleged growing threat of 'vagabonds' in Elizabethan England. A vagabond or vagrant was a poor person who travelled the country begging or looking for work.

Harman described different types of vagabond and the tricks they may have used to cheat people. For example:

- **Angler** – carried a stick with hooks to steal clothes from washing lines.
- **Clapperdudgeon** – pretended to be badly wounded by soaking dirty rags in blood and tying them around their arms and legs.
- **Doxy** – carried a large sack on her back to keep everything she has stolen.
- **Abraham man** – walked around half-naked, making strange wailing noises, pretending to be mad.

Influential

Harman's book was popular and influenced how people at the time thought about vagrants. There had always been poverty in Tudor England but Elizabeth's reign saw a dramatic rise in the numbers of poor people. Harman was a member of the gentry and he was worried about the growing number of beggars. He thought vagrants were a threat to society. Many others at the time agreed with him and Elizabeth's government introduced harsh laws to punish them.

Reflect

1 Read page 46. Link each of these four pictures to a description by Harman.

2 Read page 47. What do these people and Harman's book suggest about Elizabethan attitudes towards poverty? Explain why some people felt:

- threatened
- unsympathetic
- a duty to help.

Increased poverty

In some towns 30 per cent of the population were classed as poor. Many were children or women who had been abandoned by their husbands. Life could be awful but at least they usually had a room to stay in and could earn a little money or get help from others in the town.

Life was worse for vagrants. They were often young, unmarried men and women. They might find a job for a short period of time, for example during harvest. But many did not and they were greeted with hostility and suspicion by villagers.

Elizabethan attitudes towards poverty

Harman's book helped to stir up panic and bad feeling towards vagabonds. Historians today believe that Harman exaggerated the threat posed by vagabonds and that there was nowhere near the number of beggars as people at the time thought. However, Harman was not the only person worried about the growing numbers of poor people and the threat they might pose.

As a noble I'm expected to control the lower classes but I also have a social duty to help them. Many of my fellow landowners give food and money to the poor. But there are so many that I don't have enough money to help everyone.

As a Puritan I think that everyone should work hard to look after themselves and their families. Hard work is good for you. Not working sets a bad example to others. People who do not work are lazy. If they refuse to work, they should be punished.

As a member of the gentry I feel threatened by the growing number of poor people. Thomas Harman's book is right – beggars and vagabonds are dangerous. I hear stories of them robbing and stealing, as well as begging. I'm worried for the safety of my family. We want to feel safe in our towns and villages.

As a Justice of the Peace, I have to keep law and order in my area. Some beggars commit crimes – robbing people in the street or breaking into their homes. Some beggars ignore my orders to go away and keep coming back to a village. This is a threat to my authority. I'm also worried that these wandering groups of vagabonds will spread the plague and other diseases.

As a Privy Counsellor, I'm worried about rebellion. Elizabeth does not have a permanent army. Enemies of the Queen might persuade poor people to join a rebellion against her. This would make them even more dangerous to our government.

4.2 Reasons for the increase in poverty

Research & Record

Why did poverty become a serious problem?

1 Read the information on page 48. Sort the causes of poverty into the following categories:
- Factors that caused high unemployment
- Factors that led to low wages
- Factors that led to high food prices

Approaches to poverty	Examples from local councils
Helping the helpless 'impotent poor'	
Forcing the 'able-bodied poor' to work	
Punishing the 'idle poor' and vagabonds	

2 Read page 49. Copy and complete the above table. Find examples of the three approaches to poverty from local councils.

Factors causing increased poverty

Bad harvests caused food shortages. This meant that the price of bread and other food increased. The poor could not afford to buy food so many starved.

Changes in farming led to unemployment. Some farmers switched from growing crops to keeping sheep because wool was in high demand. They enclosed land with hedges. Sheep farming did not need so many labourers and reduced the number of jobs available in farming.

The collapse in the cloth trade meant that many weavers and spinners lost their jobs. The cloth trade was England's main industry. Woollen cloth was transported to Europe. It was a boom industry in the first half of the century but in the 1550s, just before Elizabeth became Queen, demand fell.

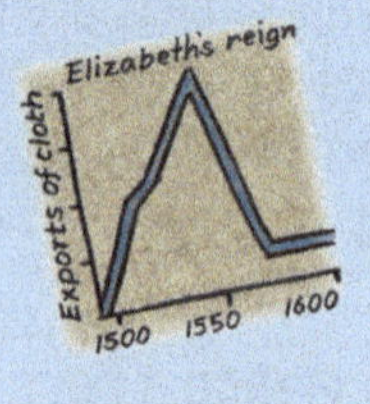

The closure of the monasteries by Henry VIII meant that many poor people were left helpless. The monasteries used to help poor people by providing food and shelter in times of hardship.

The rising population meant that there were more people looking for work. But with fewer jobs available in farming and the cloth trade, unemployment increased.

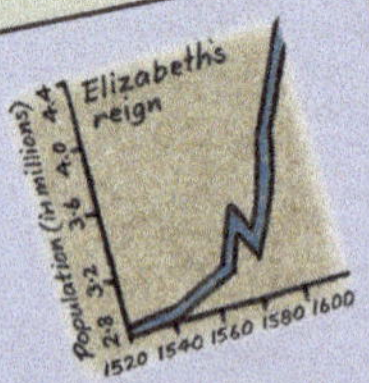

Low wages combined with high prices. With an increasing population and more workers looking for jobs, employers could pay low wages. Workers on low wages struggled to afford the rising food prices.

War meant that some people were injured and therefore could not work. At the end of Elizabeth's reign, war with Spain led to increased taxes.

Responses to poverty

Categories

Elizabethans accepted that wealthier people should take some responsibility for looking after the poor. However, they divided the poor into three categories, and treated each group differently.

Category	Who fitted into this group?	How did Elizabethans think they should be treated?
The 'impotent poor'	The 'helpless poor' who were too young, too old or too sick to work	They should be cared for and given food and a home or place to stay.
The 'able bodied poor'	People who wanted to work but had become unemployed	They were expected to work but help could be given to find them a job.
The 'idle poor'	Vagabonds, beggars and people who were able to work but chose not to	They were treated harshly – they could be whipped or forced to work in a **House of Correction**.

Local responses

Local councils responded in a variety of different ways to the growing number of poor people in their towns. Norwich and Ipswich are good examples.

◀ **SOURCE 1** A woodcut from 1577, showing vagrants being whipped

- There shall be a workplace for men to grind malt and for women to spin. The prisoners shall work for their meat and drink for at least 21 days: 15 hours a day in summer and 14 hours in winter. If they refuse to work, they will be whipped.
- One officer will go around the city each day and arrest any vagabonds.
- Beggars will be whipped six times. No person is allowed to feed or help beggars who come to their door.
- We will appoint women to take in the poorest children and women who do not work. They will learn how to read or do work.

◀ **SOURCE 2** Extracts from Norwich city records (1570–71)

- The House of Blackfriars shall become a hospital for the poor people of the town.
- The clothes-makers of this town shall set the poor to work. If any refuse to work they will be punished.
- A House of Correction* will be built.
- Young children will receive training so that they can learn a trade.

**A House of Correction was like a prison for people who refused to work.*

▶ **SOURCE 3** Extracts from Ipswich town records (1557–91)

4.3 Government action to tackle poverty

Research & Record

How did Elizabeth's government respond to the problem of poverty?

Read pages 50–1. Find examples of approaches to poverty from the national government and add them to your table.

Approaches to poverty	Examples from the national government
Helping the helpless 'impotent poor'	
Forcing the 'able-bodied poor' to work	
Punishing the 'idle poor' and vagabonds	

The reasons for government action

Elizabeth's government was slow to respond to the problem of poverty. It was often local councils that took the lead in helping the poor. Rich citizens in towns and cities like Norwich and Ipswich paid taxes to provide support. However, as it became obvious that poverty was a serious problem, Elizabeth's government introduced national laws to tackle the issue. They were worried that an increase in vagrants could lead to a rise in crime and riots and even rebellion.

By the end of Elizabeth's reign, the war with Spain had led to high taxation. This combined with poor harvests and a rising population increased the potential for social unrest. Riots broke out in London, Oxfordshire and Norfolk. Elizabeth's government knew that finding people work would reduce the threat of a major rebellion. They started to take responsibility for helping people to find work, or, if this was not possible, providing food and shelter for those in need. There was a general acceptance that this would be paid for by financial contributions from those people in work.

Examples of government action

Vagabonds Act, 1572

- Anyone found guilty of being a vagabond, over the age of 14, could be whipped and burned through the right ear.
- If the vagabond offended for a second time, they would be sent to prison. If they continued to offend when released from prison, they were to be executed.
- Local Justices of the Peace (JPs) were ordered to keep a register of the poor in their parish. They also had to raise money from local people to pay for food and shelter for sick and older people.

Act for the Relief of the Poor, 1576

- JPs were to direct the 'able-bodied poor' to find work. Those who refused would be sent to a House of Correction.

Act for the Relief of the Poor, 1598

- In each parish, four overseers of the poor were appointed. Their job was to collect money (known as a poor rate) from everyone in the parish to help the poor.
- Apprenticeships would be provided for children so that they could learn a trade.
- Hospitals would be built for older and sick people.
- The 'impotent poor' were looked after in **almshouses** which provided food, clothing and shelter.

Act for the Punishment of Vagabonds, 1598

- Vagabonds were to be whipped before being returned to their own parishes.

The Elizabethan Poor Law, 1601

All the measures on page 50 were reviewed when parliament met in 1601. The laws became known as the Elizabethan Poor Law. The laws that were introduced did not tackle the causes of poverty, and poverty continued to be a problem. More money was raised by private charity than the poor rate.

However, the actions of Elizabeth's government did help thousands of people and although there were occasional riots, the rise in poverty did not cause a rebellion.

Elizabeth's Poor Law lasted for over 200 years. Some historians have argued that Elizabeth's poor laws were too harsh and did not go far enough to help those most in need. Others have seen the Elizabethan period as an important turning point – a time when attitudes changed and it became accepted that:

- it was the government's responsibility to look after the poor
- support for the poor should be paid for by taxing those in work.

Apply ▶ Exam Practice

Question 3

Write an account of the ways in which Elizabeth's government dealt with the problem of poverty. (8 marks)

Exam Tips

Plan carefully and support your answers with specific knowledge

Plan your answer carefully. Use the Exam Tip on page 31 to help you answer this exam-style question. With 'Write an account' style questions, aim to show the **sequence of events** that took place.

- In your first paragraph – you could focus on the lack of action from Elizabeth's government at the start of her reign and how it was local councils that took the lead in responding to the problem of poverty.
- In your second paragraph – explain why and how the national government started to introduce laws to address poverty later in Elizabeth's reign.
- Demonstrate complex thinking by explaining how responses to the problem of poverty developed over time.

In the exam, you can improve your explanations by including relevant facts and precise details to support your arguments. For example, when answering this question:

- Refer to measures taken by local governments (see page 49) – explain how they show that Elizabethans treated poor people differently depending on what 'category' they belonged to.
- Refer to specific laws introduced by Elizabeth's government – explain how they show that the national government was beginning to take responsibility for helping the poor.

Summarise

1 Use these images to help you remember the reasons for increasing poverty. Check your answer on page 48.

2 Copy and complete this diagram to show the social hierarchy in Elizabethan society. Check your diagram against the diagram on page 33. Add any details you had forgotten.

Topic 5 English sailors

5.1 Reasons for exploration and colonisation

Focus on ... John Hawkins

Slave trader

Hawkins was brought up in Devon. As a young man he killed a man in a fight in a tavern.

During the 1560s, he made a lot of money from trading in enslaved people. He made three voyages from England to West Africa where he attacked Portuguese ships and captured the enslaved African people he found on board. He also took local people from their homes, and burned and raided local towns. He sold the people he captured into slavery in Spanish colonies in the Caribbean. Hawkins returned to England with gold, silver and animal skins.

Many people were keen to invest in his voyages, including Queen Elizabeth. She gave money and ships to support his voyages.

Conflict with Spain

On his third voyage, in 1568, Hawkins was joined by his young cousin, Francis Drake. By this point, Hawkins had angered the Spanish who did not allow 'unauthorised' foreigners to trade with their colonies. The Spanish attacked his fleet and Hawkins lost four ships and over 300 men. Hawkins and Drake returned to England with just 70 men. This was the last slave trading voyage for both Hawkins and Drake, but their actions had already resulted in the death and suffering of many African people. The event had a big impact on Francis Drake who was determined to get revenge for the attack. During the 1570s, Drake led attacks on Spanish colonies in Central and Southern America.

Ship designer

In 1578, Hawkins was appointed Treasurer of the English Navy and played an important role in designing new ships for the Navy. In 1588, he served as a naval commander when the Spanish Armada attacked England. The faster and more heavily armed ships that Hawkins had helped to design and build played an important role in defeating the Spanish. Hawkins was knighted for his services to the Queen.

Death

In 1595, Hawkins and Drake sailed with 27 ships to raid Spanish colonies in the Caribbean. Hawkins died the night before an unsuccessful attack on Puerto Rico.

Apology

John Hawkins made the news again in 2006, when one of his descendants publicly apologised for his ancestor's actions in the slave trade. Andrew Hawkins and 20 friends knelt in chains before 25,000 African people in a stadium in the Gambia to ask forgiveness for his ancestor's involvement in the slave trade. The Vice President of Gambia removed the chains in a show of reconciliation and forgiveness.

Reflect

Read page 52.

Explain why Hawkins played an important role in the Elizabethan era. Aim to identify and explain three consequences of his life as a sailor and ship designer.

Research & Record

What motivated English sailors to go on voyages of exploration and colonisation?

During the first half of the sixteenth century, sailors from Spain and Portugal dominated the world's seas and there had been little exploration by English sailors. Use the cause cards below to explain why English expeditions increased during Elizabeth's reign.

Aim to write three paragraphs:

- The first should cover political reasons (the chance to weaken a rival country).
- The second should cover economic factors (think of the financial benefits).
- The third should cover other factors (such as religion or adventure).

Reasons for voyages of exploration and colonisation

Cause cards

Rivalry with Spain

Spain was a Catholic country (England was Protestant) and it was the wealthiest country in Europe. England wanted to weaken Spain and challenge its power.

Spain's wealth came from gold and silver mines in what was called the **New World** (mainly Mexico and Peru). Elizabeth's government encouraged English sailors to attack and plunder Spanish ships and their territories. They hoped to gain financially and to weaken their main rival.

To the Spanish, the English sailors like Drake and Hawkins were pirates. The attacks increased tension between the two countries.

Investors and profits

Many English nobles – and even the Queen herself – invested in (paid for) overseas voyages as a way of making money. Investors and sailors like John Hawkins became very rich from brutally exploiting people in West Africa and forcing many into slavery. When Drake attacked Spanish ships carrying gold stolen from Mexico and silver from Peru in 1572 he brought home treasures worth £20,000 (over £30 million today). The investors got a share of this gold and silver. They knew they were investing in piracy but it seemed a quick and easy way to make big profits. The Spanish ships that were attacked by Drake carried gold that Spanish colonists had taken from Mexico and Peru after invading these lands and brutally exploiting the indigenous population.

The collapse of the wool and cloth trade to Europe

Demand had fallen for English wool and cloth in Europe. English merchants looked for new markets in which to sell their goods. English sailors began to explore new places that they could trade with.

English seamen were well trained and well led

Most English sailors had grown up working on the coast and had worked as merchant seamen. They were often used to smuggling or even piracy. Experienced captains such as Drake and Hawkins were successful in leading overseas voyages. They inspired great loyalty and affection from their crews, who were prepared to follow them anywhere.

Spreading Protestantism

The Elizabethans felt it was their duty to spread the Protestant religion to other countries. Elizabethan sailors, such as Walter Raleigh, believed that the Native Americans could benefit from following the religious beliefs and way of life that existed in Elizabethan England.

Adventure

Books presented sailors such as Drake as dashing heroes. They told tales of the great adventures of English sailors. The invention of the printing press enabled books to reach a wider audience.

5.2 Drake and circumnavigation, 1577–80

Research & Record

Why was Drake's circumnavigation of the world so important?

Read pages 54–5.

1 What do Drake's voyages tell us about the dangers faced by English sailors? Copy and complete the table, giving examples from Drake's circumnavigation of the world.

Dangers facing English sailors	Example
Mutiny	
Bad weather	
Attacks from local inhabitants	

2 How far did Drake achieve his aims? For each of Drake's five aims decide whether Drake:

TOTALLY SUCCEEDED | PARTIALLY SUCCEEDED | FAILED

Drake's circumnavigation of the world

Drake was an experienced sailor. At the age of 12 he had become an apprentice on a trade ship and in his early 20s he had begun travelling to the Americas with his cousin, Sir John Hawkins. During the 1570s Drake raided Spanish colonies and ships in Central America and the Caribbean.

By November 1577 he had planned his most daring and dangerous mission yet, to sail all the way round (circumnavigate) the world. As you can see from the map on page 55, it took him three years but he succeeded.

Drake's aims and motives

1 **Glory –** Drake wanted to impress the Queen. Elizabeth sponsored Drake's voyage to circumnavigate the Earth. Drake hoped to find new lands to claim for the Queen. This would make England more powerful.

2 **Revenge –** Drake wanted revenge for the Spanish attack on Hawkins' fleet in 1568. He planned to attack Spanish colonies in Central America from the Pacific side, where defences were weaker.

3 **Religion –** Drake was a Puritan and wanted to weaken the greatest Catholic power in Europe. A weaker Spain would also make England more secure from attack.

4 **Money –** Drake aimed to capture Spanish gold, silver and other treasure, both to make money for himself and to reward courtiers who had invested in his expedition.

5 **Trade –** Drake wanted to establish new and better trade routes and find new markets where English merchants could sell their goods overseas. Several merchants helped to finance Drake's voyage.

The consequences of Drake's voyage

1 **Glory** – Drake was treated as a national hero. He was the first Englishman to sail around the world. The Queen knighted him aboard his ship, the *Golden Hind*.

2 **Revenge** – Drake challenged Spain's dominance of America. His success encouraged other sailors to do the same.

3 **Religion –** Philip II had supported Catholic plots to overthrow Elizabeth. Drake's actions weakened Spain and helped to reduce the threat of a Catholic take-over.

4 **Money –** He brought back gold, silver and jewels worth around £140,000 (about £200 million today). Drake's investors were delighted. The Queen's share (about half the money) was more than her entire income for a whole year.

5 **Trade** – Drake claimed new lands for England and made valuable trading contacts with the Spice Islands (the Moluccas – a group of islands to the north-east of Indonesia).

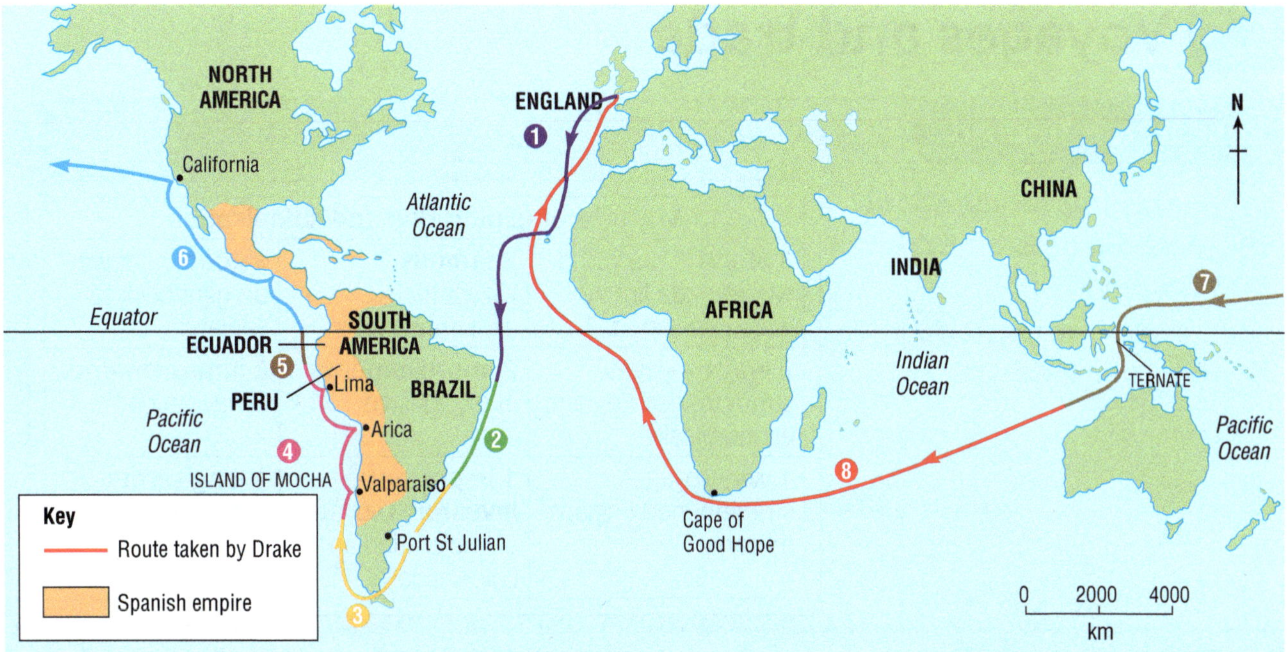

Stage 1: December 1577

Drake set sail from Plymouth with five ships and around 170 men. He sailed to the west coast of **Africa**, where he attacked Spanish and Portuguese ships before setting off across the Atlantic Ocean.

Stage 2: Spring and summer 1578

The fleet sailed down the coast of **Brazil**. By this point, serious quarrels had broken out among his crew. Drake's former friend, Sir Thomas Doughty was charged with mutiny and executed. Drake then put all his men and stores on to his three best ships, and burnt the others.

Stage 3: September 1578 – January 1579

In September, Drake's remaining three ships reached the Pacific Ocean and made their way up the west coast of South America. No English sailor had been there before. They were hit by stormy weather which lasted for about a month. The *Marigold* sank and the *Elizabeth* got lost, but eventually managed to find her way back to England. Drake was left with just one ship, which was running low on food and water. When he landed on the island of **Mocha** to take on water, he was attacked by its inhabitants. Drake was wounded by arrows on his face and head.

Stage 4: February 1579

After they recovered, Drake and the crew attacked Spanish colonies along the coast of **Peru**. The Spanish were taken by surprise and Drake captured gold, Spanish coins, silver, silks and supplies of wine.

Stage 5: March 1579

Near the coast of **Ecuador**, Drake attacked the *Cacafuego*, a Spanish treasure ship. This was Drake's most famous gain as the ship contained a large quantity of gold, silver and jewels.

Stage 6: June 1579

By now, Drake had only one ship and about 55 men. He landed in **California** and claimed it for Queen Elizabeth, naming it Nova Albion (New England).

Stage 7: November 1579

From California, Drake sailed west across the Pacific Ocean, eventually landing in **Ternate**, famous for its spices. Drake made a trade treaty with the king of the island, which allowed English merchants to trade in spices. His ship was loaded up with tons of cloves, ginger and pepper.

Stage 8: January – September 1580

Drake set off on the long journey home, sailing across the Indian Ocean, past the **Cape of Good Hope** and up the coast of West Africa. In September 1580, Drake finally arrived back in Plymouth, his ship packed with treasure.

5.3 Voyages and trade

Research & Record

What was important about the voyages of exploration and colonisation?

Find examples from pages 56–7 to fill in a bingo card like this one.

Voyages of exploration and colonisation		
3 areas of the world where trade links were developed	**3 famous** Elizabethan explorers/sailors	**3 goods** that were brought back to England
2 ways voyages strengthened England economically	**2 improvements** in ship design	**2 improvements** in navigation
1 way voyages strengthened England militarily	**1 important investor** in voyages of exploration and colonisation	**1 long-term consequence** of the voyages

Trading companies

English sailors did not just aim to damage Spain by attacking their colonies and ships. They also set up important trade routes with other parts of the world. The map below shows where trading companies were set up.

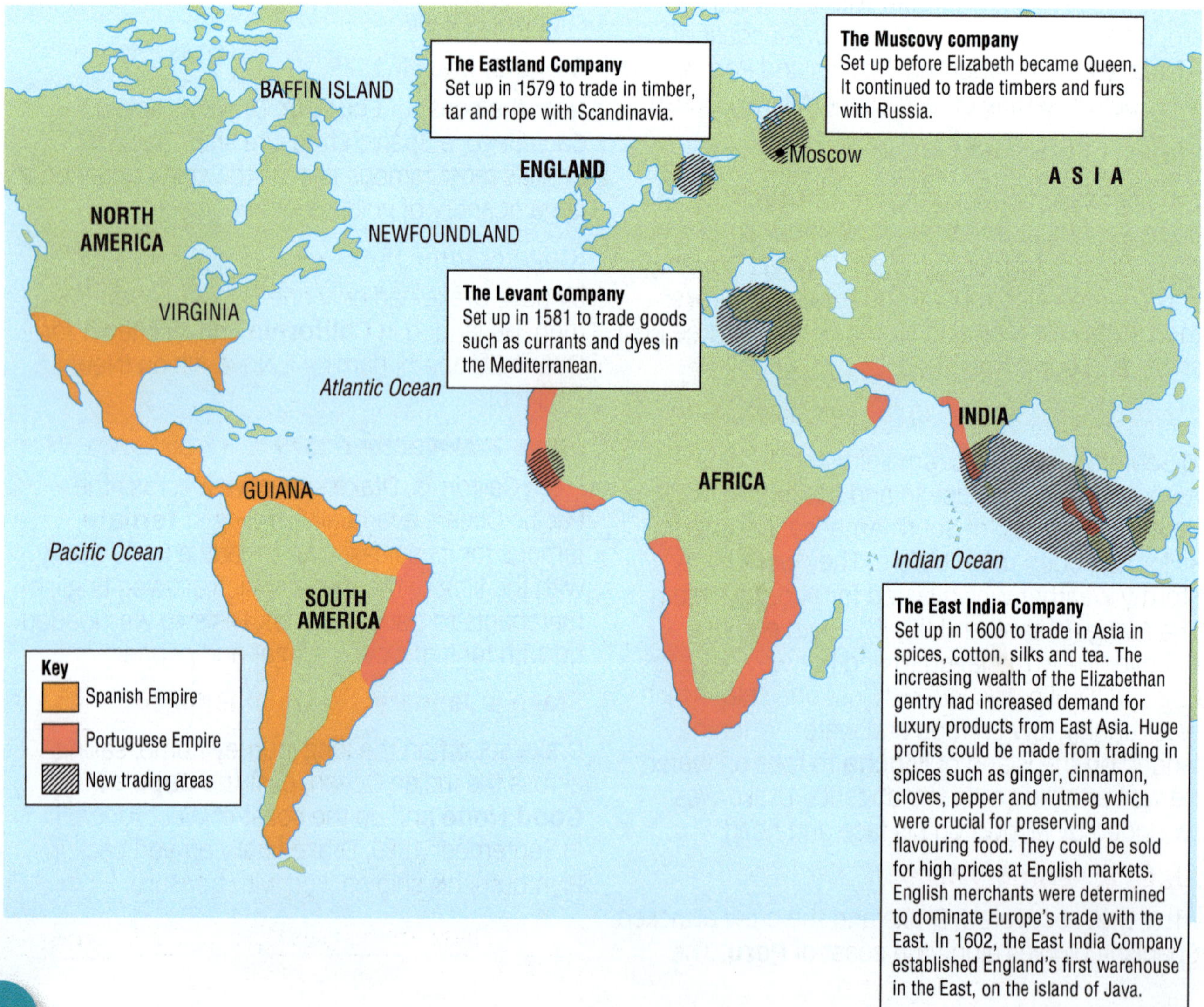

How were the voyages possible?

Improved ship design and navigation tools meant that sailors could make longer voyages than ever before.

Navigation

- **Better maps and sea charts** showing the parallels of latitude and longitude made it easier for English sailors to navigate around the world.
- The **printing press** meant that these maps became available in large numbers.
- The development of the **magnetic compass** improved navigation and was particularly useful for measuring longitude (how far east or west you were).
- The **astrolabe** allowed sailors to work out their latitude (how far north or south they were) by measuring the angle between the horizon and the North Star. This meant that a ship's position could be plotted correctly.

Ship design

- **Improved sails** led to stronger and faster ships that could carry more goods home to England. Ships were now fitted with **triangular sails**, which could easily be turned to catch the strong winds of the open seas. This cut journey times and allowed ships to sail in any direction.
- **Improved rudders** gave the crew more control in steering ships.
- Ships could be fitted out with the latest artillery, including the more **rapid-firing guns**. English sailors could target Spanish treasure ships.

Summarise

How did England benefit from the voyages of exploration and colonisation?

When you revise, it is important to be able to identify the big points and connect them to topics you have already covered and new topics that are coming up. And the more often you revisit the important content the more ways you will have to remember it.

The summary table below identifies three 'big' consequences of the voyages and connects them to important events that you will go on to study. Complete your own copy of the table, using your knowledge of what we have covered in this chapter so far.

Benefit	Link to what you already know	Link to later events
1 A stronger economy	*Improved trade links made many merchants and investors very wealthy.* *Investors made large profits from cargoes of gold and silver captured from Spanish ships by sailors such as …* *England's economy had been struggling because of a fall in demand for …* *But Elizabethan sailors helped to set up profitable trade links with countries such as …*	The new trading companies became very wealthy and powerful in the seventeenth century. During this period English merchants developed new and brutal ways of making money. England became the world's biggest slave-trading country and built up slave-powered colonies in the Caribbean and America. These colonies were places where millions of African people were taken and forced to work in horrific conditions. grew a trade in human beings that made England the world's biggest slave-trading country.
2 A stronger navy	*The voyages improved the skills of English sail-ors. They gained experience of fighting at sea and started to make full use of new technology such as …*	Faster ships equipped with quick-firing cannon helped to defeat the Spanish Armada in 1588 (see Chapter 8).
3 The beginnings of an empire	*Spain had built up a large empire in …* *During the Elizabethan period, English sailors started to challenge the dominance of Spanish sailors. For example, …*	Sailors such as Walter Raleigh (see pages 58–9) tried to set up colonies overseas during Elizabeth's reign. Although they did not succeed, they laid the foundations and during the seventeenth century, colonies were established in Africa, India and North America. These colonies grew into the British Empire.

5.4 The role of Raleigh

Research & Record

How important was the role of Sir Walter Raleigh?

1. Read page 58. What does Raleigh's relationship with Elizabeth tell us about the royal court and Elizabeth's character?
2. Read page 59. Why did Elizabeth and her government support Raleigh's expeditions?
3. Raleigh failed to establish a colony in North America. Does this mean that his role was not important? Explain your answer.

Raleigh's relationship with Elizabeth

Favourite

Walter Raleigh's dashing and flamboyant character caught Elizabeth's attention when he started to attend the royal court. He quickly became one of the Queen's favourite courtiers. He was very loyal to Elizabeth, spending time in Ireland fighting Catholics who had rebelled against her. Elizabeth knighted him and he was also given a lot of land in England and Ireland as a reward.

Sailor

During the 1580s, Raleigh persuaded Elizabeth to agree to an expedition to the coast of North America, which he would name Virginia, in her honour (Elizabeth was known as the Virgin Queen). Raleigh wanted to build an English empire to rival those of Spain and Portugal. He was responsible for planning, organising and financing two voyages that sailed to America in 1585 and 1587. Elizabeth did not let Raleigh join the expeditions as she wanted him at court. Both expeditions ran into problems and Raleigh was not able to establish a permanent **colony** in North America. You can find out why on pages 60–1.

Banned

In the summer of 1592, Raleigh angered Elizabeth when she found out that he had secretly married her maid of honour, Bess Throckmorton. Bess had hidden her pregnancy from Elizabeth and given birth to a baby boy. Elizabeth sent both Raleigh and Bess to the Tower of London. They were released after a few months but Raleigh was banned from court and had to wait five years before the Queen would speak to him again. Bess was never allowed to return to court.

Search for the city of gold

Raleigh was desperate to please the Queen and regain his important position within Elizabeth's court. In 1595, he led an expedition to South America. He was hoping to find El Dorado, a legendary city full of gold. He reached Guiana but did not find El Dorado.

Why did Raleigh try to build a colony in North America?

Elizabeth was often a cautious and careful leader. As you will see, establishing a colony in North America would be difficult and dangerous. However, the Queen and her government saw many advantages in encouraging expeditions to North America.

We must stop rival, Catholic countries such as Spain and France from settling there. This is our chance to spread the Protestant religion. Spain is already spreading Catholicism in central and southern America.

We can increase England's power by taking over more territory. Having our own colonies will make us more respected by other countries.

We need a military base from where English forces can raid Spanish colonies in the Caribbean and attack Spanish treasure ships.

England's population is growing quickly. We need people to emigrate. North America could offer a better life for poor people in England.

We need new trade links. A colony in this area could provide oil, wine and sugar. Raleigh tells us that this area is home to friendly and 'civilised' Native Americans, has fertile land and is full of animals that can be hunted for food.

The consequences of Raleigh's expeditions

Raleigh's expeditions did not establish a long-lasting colony in North America (you can find out why on the next page), nor did they find cities full of gold, but they did have longer term importance:

- In 1596, Raleigh published a popular book about his expeditions, *The Discovery of the Large, Rich and Beautiful Empire of Guiana*. Its tales of riches encouraged other sailors to build an English empire overseas.
- They increased knowledge of North America.
- Merchants saw opportunities to build trade links with North America.
- They laid the foundations for the colonisation of America by English colonists in the sixteenth century.

5.5 Case study: The 1585 and 1587 expeditions to North America

Research & Record

Why did Raleigh struggle to establish a permanent colony in North America?

Read pages 60–1. Copy and complete the table to record your findings. Aim to identify at least two main reasons/causes.

Identify a reason	Support with examples	Explain why this created a problem
Bad weather	In 1585, a bad storm meant that only one ship made it to America. In 1587, hurricanes ...	The colonists lost most of their supplies. This meant that ...

1585: An abandoned colony

Elizabeth would not allow Raleigh to leave the royal court, so the 1585 voyage to America was led by Sir Richard Grenville and Ralph Lane.

Storms

The expedition was carefully planned, with seven ships carrying 600 sailors, soldiers and colonists. But crossing the Atlantic was difficult and after just five days, the fleet of ships was scattered by a fierce storm. Only Grenville's ship sailed on.

Sandbanks

When his ship reached North America, it got stuck on sandbanks just as a storm approached. The colonists lost most of their supplies, including the seeds they had brought to plant.

Settlement

Grenville decided to return to England to get more colonists and supplies, while Lane stayed behind with just over 100 men to build a fort and colony on Roanoke Island.

Starvation

At first, relations between the English colonists and the local Native American population were good. Wingina, the Algonquian chief who ruled the area, supplied the colonists with corn but during the winter his own people started to run out of food for their families. Lane heard that Wingina was planning to attack the colony. He decided to attack first and Wingina was killed.

Escape or rescue

The English colonists feared a revenge attack and their food supplies were running very low. In June 1586, they were forced to abandon the colony they had built on the island. Lane and his men were rescued and taken home by Francis Drake who had arrived at the colony on his way home from the Caribbean (then known as the West Indies).

▲ **SOURCE 1** A 1590 engraving of the arrival of the English in Virginia, by Theodor de Bry

1587: A second attempt

On his return to Court, Ralph Lane suggested that Chesapeake Bay would be a better place for a colony than Roanoke. Lane believed it would be the ideal base from which to search for gold in North America. Raleigh was given permission by the Queen to send a second expedition, led by John White.

Wrong place

Once again, the expedition did not go as planned. The ship's master pilot was worried about hurricanes and dropped the colonists off on Roanoke Island, refusing to take them any further. The local Native Americans remained suspicious and hostile towards the colonists. They had been attacked by the colonists in 1585 and they did not want the colonists taking good land and important resources.

Pirates

White was badly in need of supplies and decided to return to England. On the journey, his ship was attacked by French pirates and White was badly injured fighting them off.

Delay

When White finally arrived in England he was told that all ships were needed to defend England against an attack from the Spanish Armada.

The mystery of the missing colonists

White did not return to Roanoke until 1590. When he arrived, he must have hoped and prayed that the colony had survived. His daughter Eleanor, her husband and his young granddaughter were among the colonists he had dropped off in 1587.

Sadly, as he explored the island, no one answered his calls. White found that a new fort had been erected but the houses of the colony had been taken down and removed. No members of the colony could be found.

White found the letters 'CRO' carved into a tree and thought that the colonists might have moved to live with the local Croatoan people to the south of Roanoke. White tried to sail south to look for them but stormy weather forced his ship further and further north until there was no option but to return home. The settlers were never found.

What happened to the colonists remains a mystery.

- The English colonists may have been attacked and killed by local people.
- Another explanation for the colonists' disappearance is starvation. White had returned to England because supplies were low and local people may have been unwilling to share food during the winter months.

Part 2: Life in Elizabethan times review

Reflect

The Elizabethan period is often referred to as a 'Golden Age'. What do you think? Is this a convincing interpretation? In other words, is it supported by strong evidence?

Produce a table in which you record the evidence for and against a Golden Age.

Demonstrate complex thinking – use criteria to help you reach a judgement.

- Was it a **political** Golden Age? A time of stability and effective government?
- Was it an **economic** Golden Age? A time of new trade links and increased wealth and prosperity?
- Was it a **cultural** Golden Age? A time when music, literature, theatre and architecture flourished?

Discuss and debate these questions with other students. It will help you test the strength of your arguments.

Apply Recall Challenges

Revisiting Part 1

Remember it is important to regularly revisit what you have learnt. Look back at the Recall Challenges at the end of Part 1 (see page 30). Try these again from memory alone before you look them up.

Testing yourself on Part 2

Know your key words

Make a large copy of this bingo card. Use an A4 piece of paper, so you have plenty of space to write in each box. Write a definition of each word from memory. Then check with the glossary on page 94.

Key word		
gentry	vagabond	astrolabe
merchant	impotent poor	circumnavigation
yeomen	nobles	colony

For each event, try to answer from memory:

- **When** did this happen?
- **What** happened?
- **Why** did this happen? What motivated those involved?
- **So what?** What were the consequences. Why did it have an important impact on Elizabethan society?

Know your key events

- Hardwick Hall was built.
- The Globe Theatre was built.
- The Elizabethan Poor Law was introduced.
- Drake sailed round the world.
- Raleigh's sent expeditions to North America.

Summarise

1 Use the **5Ps** + **3Ps** memory aid to recall:
- Five reasons why theatres were built during the Elizabethan period
- Three reasons why some people opposed the theatre.

You can check your answer by looking back to page 43.

2 Look at this memory aid. His 'STACK' (pile) of achievements will help you to remember why Sir Francis Drake was important.

Apply Exam Practice

Question 1: How convincing?

How convincing is Interpretation A about what happened when Raleigh's men tried to establish a colony at Roanoke?

Explain your answer using Interpretation A and your contextual knowledge. (8 marks)

▲ **Interpretation A** An illustration of what happened at Roanoke in 1585–86 (the first expedition). It appeared on the front page of the magazine *Look and Learn* in 1962

Question 2: Explain importance

Explain what was important about the voyages of exploration and colonisation that took place during the Elizabethan period. (8 marks)

3 Develop your own similar memory aid for Sir Walter Raleigh. For example you could use this acronym
F = favourite courtier
A = America (Virginia)
M = Marriage (displeased the Queen)
E = El Dorado (failed expedition and the book he wrote)

Exam Tips

Question 1: Evaluating interpretations

Look again at the advice on how to approach this type of question on page 31.

Remember to **start by focusing on the content of the interpretation**. Look carefully for clues in the interpretation and use your inference skills.

- What is being suggested about the relationship between Raleigh's men and the Native Americans?
- How is Roanoke portrayed? Does the colony look successful and well organised? Do Raleigh's men look in control?

Then **use your own knowledge of this topic to evaluate** this message.

- In one paragraph you could make the point that at first, relations between the colonists and local people were good. Give examples to show this.
- In your second paragraph you could challenge the messages in the interpretation – explaining that relations did not remain positive and that the colonists struggled to survive (remember that they ended up having to be rescued).

End by reaching a **clear overall judgement** on the extent to which the message given in the interpretation is convincing. Is it very convincing or only partly convincing?

Question 2: Developing strong explanations

You should aim to produce two paragraphs – each paragraph should start with a clear reason why the voyages were important.

- One paragraph could focus on the economic importance (give specific examples of trade links that were developed and the amount of wealth that was captured from Spanish ships).
- The second paragraph could focus on political/military importance – how the voyages started to challenge the dominance of Spain (England's main rival) and mark the beginnings of an empire.

Remember to support **and** develop the points you make. Look again at the advice on page 15 to help you.

Topic 6 Religious matters

6.1 The question of religion, English Catholicism and Protestantism

Focus on … Sir Francis Walsingham

The spymaster

The serious-looking man on the right of this picture, just behind Queen Elizabeth, is Sir Francis Walsingham. He played a very important role within Elizabeth's government. He became head of a spy network which aimed to hunt down Catholics that were a threat to Elizabeth.

Walsingham became Secretary of State and a member of the Queen's Privy Council in 1572. He saw it as his God-given role to protect Elizabeth from harm. Walsingham organised a network of spies and informers to keep an eye on all suspected Catholics and track down priests in hiding.

He was ruthlessly efficient. Nearly 200 Catholics were executed. He was able to plant his spies deep within the Catholic community and he was prepared to torture captured priests and plotters in order to find out about threats to Elizabeth. Some Catholic priests chose to become secret informers for Walsingham's spy network, rather than face an agonising death.

Escape to Italy

Walsingham was a Puritan and had a deep hatred of Catholicism. His father had been a lawyer and a member of the Norfolk gentry but he died when Francis was very young, leaving him in the care of his mother's family. His uncle was close to Henry VIII and a keen supporter of Protestantism. When Mary I became Queen, Walsingham refused to accept the return of Catholicism. He left the country to study in Italy. He must have been horrified when he heard stories of Protestants being burned at the stake back home in England.

Return to England

Walsingham returned home after Elizabeth became Queen. He became a Member of Parliament and a few years later began working for Elizabeth's government. Elizabeth thought that his Puritan religious views and hatred of Catholics was too extreme. However, he could speak French and Italian, and had good contacts abroad which made him very useful to her. In 1571, Walsingham helped to uncover a Catholic plot against Elizabeth that involved the Pope and Spain.

In 1572, Walsingham was serving as ambassador to Paris when he witnessed the St Bartholomew's Day massacres. Protestants were attacked and killed in the city. Walsingham believed that Catholics were a threat to England's security and his fears increased when Catholic priests began to arrive in England, with the aim of spreading their religion. Walsingham responded by persuading parliament to pass stricter laws against Catholics.

Reflect

1 Read page 64. What events shaped Walsingham's beliefs and influenced his actions?
2 Read page 65. Which parts of Elizabeth's Religious Settlement would Walsingham have been happy with? Which parts would he have been unhappy with? Explain why.

The Elizabethan Religious Settlement

Elizabeth could not please everyone with her religious policies. People in the sixteenth century had very strong religious views and many were prepared to die for their religious beliefs. Protestants, Puritans and Catholics all had very different views about the key religious questions. The table below summarises these disagreements and Elizabeth's solution, which became known as the Elizabethan Religious Settlement.

Areas of disagreement	Catholic beliefs	Protestant beliefs	Puritan beliefs	Elizabeth's solution
Who should be head of the Church?	Catholics believed that the Pope should be head of the Church. Cardinals, archbishops and bishops would help him to govern the Church.	Protestants did not accept the authority of the Pope. Instead, they thought that the monarch should be head of the Church. Archbishops and bishops would help the monarch govern the Church.	Puritans were Protestants who had extreme views about how the Church should change. They did not believe in a head of the Church or bishops, and wanted committees elected by churchgoers to make the rules.	The Act of Supremacy (1559) stated that Elizabeth was the Supreme Governor of the Church in England.
What should churches look like?	Catholic churches were filled with decorations such as stained-glass windows, huge altars, statues and pictures.	Protestants believed that expensive churches went against the teachings of Jesus. Edward VI ordered that all Catholic decorations be removed from churches.	Puritans wanted very simple churches – with white-washed walls, no stained-glass windows and plain tables instead of altars.	Elizabeth kept decoration and ornaments in churches. The Puritans did not get their wish for simple-looking churches.
Should the Bible and church services be in Latin or English?	Catholics wanted church services and the Bible to be in Latin.	Protestants wanted church services and the Bible to be in English, which everyone could read.	Puritans also wanted the Bible to be in English. They wanted simple church services with the minister dressed in plain black robes.	The Act of Uniformity (1559) said that all worship should be the same (uniform). Each week, everyone had to attend a church service that followed the Book of Common Prayer in English. If not they had to pay a fine. Priests had to wear religious robes.

Elizabeth's aims

Elizabeth had been brought up as a Protestant and did not want the Pope to have any authority over religion in England. However, Elizabeth's views about Catholics were not as strong as those of people such as Francis Walsingham. She was willing to compromise. Elizabeth kept the Church hierarchy and some features of Catholicism that she liked.

Elizabeth's main aim was to unite the country. She knew that disagreements over religion could split the country and lead to rebellion. She did not want people with different beliefs to be punished. Elizabeth intended to let Catholicism in England die out slowly. She knew that trying to stamp it out immediately could create unrest, protest and rebellion.

The majority of people, including most priests, accepted these changes and there were no protests or major rebellions in the early part of Elizabeth's reign.

6.2 The Northern Rebellion

Research & Record

What were the causes of the Northern Rebellion, and why did it fail?

1 The Northern Rebellion was partly about **religion**, but it was also about **politics** and the **succession** (who would be monarch after Elizabeth). Use evidence from the cause cards on page 67 to prove that all three factors played a role in causing the rebellion.

2 Why did the rebellion fail? Use the information on pages 66–7 to find and record evidence of the following factors:
- Poor leadership
- Timing (mid-winter)
- Lack of support
- A strong response from Elizabeth and her government

Background

In 1569, a serious rebellion broke out in the north of England. It was led by the Earls of Northumberland and Westmorland who were both leading Catholic nobles. They supported a plan for the Duke of Norfolk to marry Mary Queen of Scots and to set her up as Elizabeth's heir. Norfolk thought that this would weaken Cecil's position at court and strengthen his own. Norfolk had no plan to remove Elizabeth but when she found out about what Norfolk and his supporters were planning, she was furious. Norfolk was captured and imprisoned.

He begged for the Queen's forgiveness and ordered his supporters not to carry out a rebellion. Elizabeth ordered Norfolk's supporters, including the Earls of Northumberland and Westmorland, to court. The Earls must have feared for their lives. They may have thought that their only option was to rebel.

The causes of the rebellion

Elizabeth's Religious Settlement. The rebels wanted to restore the Catholic faith. They opposed Elizabeth's Religious Settlement. They believed that Elizabeth's 'evil' Privy Counsellors had persuaded Elizabeth to change the Church from Catholic to Protestant.

Elizabeth's treatment of Mary Queen of Scots. Elizabeth had placed her Catholic cousin under arrest when she arrived in England. The rebels thought this unfair.

Elizabeth had taken away some of the Earls' power in the north of England. Elizabeth did not trust the Earls because of their Catholic faith and she had placed her own followers in positions of power in the north of England. This angered the Earls who believed that they should have the right to continue to dominate the area.

The Earls felt they had lost influence at the royal court. Elizabeth had taken land away from the Earls. Northumberland had lost valuable copper mines.

The Earls believed that Elizabeth's counsellors had too much influence – particularly William Cecil. They blamed Cecil for their loss of political power.

Support from abroad. Philip II of Spain and the Pope appeared to be willing to support the rebellion.

What happened?

1 A group of 5000 rebels gathered at **Brancepeth** Castle. These rebels put loyalty to their local lords before their loyalty to Queen Elizabeth. They wore Catholic badges and emblems.

2 The rebels marched to **Durham**, which was one of the most important cities in northern England. It was not well defended. The Protestant bishop fled the city with his family disguised as beggars. The rebels destroyed Protestant prayer books then celebrated the traditional Catholic Mass in Latin in the Cathedral.

3 The rebels then marched south. They captured **Barnard Castle** and the port of **Hartlepool**. They had been promised that Spanish forces would arrive there to help them but no one ever came.

4 They hoped to gather support from other Catholics in the North. They asked Catholic nobles in **Lancashire and Cheshire** for help but they refused to join the revolt. Important towns such as **York** and **Pontefract** remained in the control of government forces.

5 Elizabeth's government responded quickly and efficiently. The Duke of Sussex led 10,000 soldiers northwards. When the rebel leaders heard about the size and strength of the royal army they panicked and retreated north across the **River Tees** and into Scotland. The rebellion was over.

6 Northumberland was handed over by the Scots and beheaded at York in 1572. Westmorland escaped abroad. A total of 450 other rebels were executed.

The consequences of the rebellion

Elizabeth ordered the execution of 700 rebels, although the number actually executed was probably nearer 450. The Privy Council demanded that the Duke of Norfolk be executed as well but, out of family loyalty (he was a second cousin of Elizabeth), she had the Duke imprisoned in the Tower of London. He was released after nine months.

Elizabeth strengthened her control of the north of England by confiscating land belonging to the rebels.

The rebellion encouraged the government to take firmer action over the issue of religion. The Act of Uniformity was more strictly enforced and stricter laws were introduced against Catholics.

6.3 Elizabeth's excommunication and the arrival of Catholic missionaries

Research & Record

How did Catholics respond to the Elizabethan Religious Settlement?

1 Read pages 68–9 and use the information to copy and complete the table. Aim to explain how the events in column 1 changed Catholic attitudes towards Elizabeth and her religious policies. Use column 2 to explain them fully.

2 Read page 69. Write a paragraph explaining how Walsingham responded to some Catholics turning against Elizabeth. Make sure you include the **3 Is: I**nterception, **I**nformers and **I**nterrogation.

Turning point	Explanation – How did this change Catholic attitudes?
The arrival of Mary Queen of Scots	This gave Catholics hope that there was a Catholic alternative to Elizabeth. Mary had a strong claim to the throne.
Elizabeth's excommunication	
The arrival of Catholic missionaries	

Catholic reactions to the Elizabethan Religious Settlement

Most Catholics accepted Elizabeth's Settlement but some did not. The four reactions are summarised below.

- **Conformers** – Many Catholics dropped their old faith and became Protestants.
- **Church papists** – Most English Catholics kept their Catholic beliefs but attended Protestant church services. If they kept their Catholic beliefs but did nothing to challenge Elizabeth's position, she was happy with this. She allowed Catholics to attend court and at the beginning of her reign she did not even strictly enforce laws about church attendance.
- **Recusants** – Several thousand Catholics refused to attend Protestant church services, and the number started to rise during the 1580s. The fines for not attending a Protestant church service were high.
- **Plotters** – A small number of Catholics plotted against the Queen. They felt that it was their duty to God and the Pope to overthrow Elizabeth and replace her with Mary Queen of Scots.

Elizabeth's excommunication

In February 1570, Pope Pius V issued a **papal bull** (decree) of excommunication against Elizabeth. This expelled Elizabeth from the Roman Catholic Church. In doing this, the Pope was showing late support for the 1569 Northern Rebellion. He was also sending a clear message to all English Catholics that they no longer had to obey Elizabeth. This made it easier for Catholics in England and foreign rulers to plot to overthrow Elizabeth. It also led to the arrival of enthusiastic, young missionaries from Europe, determined to spread Catholicism in England.

The arrival of Catholic missionaries

In the mid-1570s, an increased number of Catholic priests secretly arrived in England from France. These young English Catholics had been trained abroad in France and Italy. The priests were trained to support Catholics in England but were told not to try and persuade Protestants to become Catholics.

Jesuit

More of a threat to Elizabeth was the arrival of **Jesuit** missionaries from Europe. Jesuit priests were totally loyal to the Pope and specially trained to persuade people either to become Catholics or to show a stronger Catholic faith. Their aim was to gain influence over rich and powerful families, turning them against the Queen.

Hiding places

From 1580, Jesuits were smuggled into England in disguise and secretly stayed in the country houses of wealthy Catholic families. Some Catholic families in the gentry created secret hiding places called 'priest holes' in tiny spaces behind walls or below floorboards where Jesuit priests might hide for days with very little food and water.

Increased threat

From 1580, there was also a significant rise in the number of **recusants** who refused to attend church. More Catholics were disobeying the laws and this represented a threat to Elizabeth's authority. Plots against the Queen also increased (see pages 70–1). Elizabeth's government responded by introducing stricter laws against Catholics (see page 72) and establishing a spy network under the supervision of Francis Walsingham.

Summarise

The role played by Walsingham and his spy network

By the 1580s, Elizabeth's Secretary of State, Sir Francis Walsingham, had built up an effective network of informers and spies. Their brief was to find out about the movements of Catholic priests and uncover any plots to overthrow Elizabeth. Walsingham's agents used a range of methods. They can be remembered by the **3 Is**. Think of Walsingham's eyes being everywhere.

6.4 Catholic plots and the threat to the Elizabethan Settlement

Research & Record

How dangerous was the threat posed to Elizabeth by Catholic plots?

1 Read pages 70–1 and copy and complete the table below.

Plot	When?	Who was behind it?	Aims of the plotters	What happened?
Ridolfi Plot	1571	Mary Queen of Scots, the Pope, Philip II	Invade England and replace Elizabeth with Mary	
Throckmorton Plot				
Babington Plot				

2 Which plot represented the biggest threat to Elizabeth? Explain your answer using the criteria below:
- Who was involved and how powerful were they?
- How well planned was the plot?
- How close did it come to success?

3 Was this plot more dangerous than the Northern Rebellion? Look back at pages 66–7 and use the criteria above to help you explain your answer.

The threats to the Elizabethan Settlement

The Northern Rebellion highlighted the danger of Catholic plots against Elizabeth. As you have already seen on pages 68–9, three key events (turning points) also added to the danger.

▲ **SOURCE 1** A drawing of the Pope issuing the bull in 1570 that excommunicated Elizabeth. The Pope was involved in the Ridolfi Plot to overthrow Elizabeth

- The arrival of Mary Queen of Scots in England (1568)
- Elizabeth's excommunication from the Catholic Church (1570)
- The arrival of Catholic missionaries from Europe (1570s)

Between 1571 and 1585 there were three serious Catholic plots against Elizabeth as well as assassination attempts.

The Ridolfi Plot (1571)

- Roberto Ridolfi was an Italian banker used by Mary Queen of Scots to carry messages to the Pope and Philip II of Spain.
- Mary and the Duke of Norfolk wanted the Pope and Spain to join forces and organise an invasion of England that would overthrow Elizabeth. Ridolfi thought that this could be achieved by the arrival of around 6000 Spanish troops, who would be joined by Catholics in England. Mary would become Queen, marry the Duke of Norfolk and restore Catholicism.
- Ridolfi met with the Duke of Alva, the commander of the Spanish armies in the Netherlands. However, Alva was wary of leading an invasion. He suggested to Philip II that Spain should only invade after Elizabeth had been overthrown.
- A coded document, outlining the invasion plan was left with the Duke of Norfolk but the plot was uncovered. Norfolk was arrested and executed for treason. Parliament put pressure on Elizabeth to have Mary Queen of Scots executed as well but Elizabeth refused.

The Throckmorton Plot (1583)

- This plot planned an uprising of English Catholic nobles to free Mary Queen of Scots, make her Queen of England and restore Catholicism.
- Francis Throckmorton was a young English Catholic who carried letters between Mary Queen of Scots and the French and Spanish ambassadors. He was also in contact with members of the English Catholic nobility.
- Throckmorton was put under surveillance and then arrested. When his house was searched, papers were found that showed that Throckmorton and leading Catholic nobles were planning an uprising in the north of England to happen at the same time as an invasion led by the French Duke of Guise with financial support from Spain and the Pope.
- Throckmorton claimed that the money he had been promised by the Spanish ambassador never arrived. When interrogated, Throckmorton also stated that Mary Queen of Scots was fully aware of the plot. He later withdrew this claim, saying that he had made this statement under torture.

The Babington Plot (1586)

- Anthony Babington was another young Catholic who carried letters for Mary Queen of Scots. He was encouraged by his Catholic friends to support a plot to invade England, kill Elizabeth and place Mary Queen of Scots on the throne.
- A Catholic priest was behind the plot but he was being watched by government agents.
- By this point, England was at war with Spain and the threat of invasion was very real. Once again, the plot was uncovered by Elizabeth's government. Spies, working as double agents, had been placed within Mary's household. They persuaded Mary that it was safe to receive and send letters hidden in beer barrels. All the letters were intercepted and sent to Walsingham, including one in which Mary agreed to the assassination of Elizabeth.
- Those involved in the plot, including Babington, were arrested and found guilty of treason. They were executed in September 1586. In the same month, Mary Queen of Scots was placed on trial, and was found guilty of plotting to take Elizabeth's life. Eventually, Elizabeth was persuaded to sign her death warrant. Mary Queen of Scots was executed in February 1587.

6.5 The response of Elizabeth's government to the Catholic threat

Research & Record

How did Elizabeth's government respond to the Catholic threat?

Read pages 72–3. Find and record three examples to support each of the following statements.

- Financial punishments increased.
- Physical punishments, including torture and executions, increased.

The consequences of the Catholic plots

Philip II and the Spanish ambassador had been involved in a number of the plots against Elizabeth and this damaged the relationship between England and Spain. After the Throckmorton Plot, Elizabeth expelled the Spanish ambassador from England.

English Catholics involved in the plots (including Throckmorton and Babington) were executed. The Duke of Norfolk, a leading Protestant noble, was also executed for his role in plots against Elizabeth.

Walsingham and other leading counsellors came to believe that Elizabeth would never be safe as long as Mary Queen of Scots was alive. Eventually, after the Babington Plot, Elizabeth agreed to sign Mary's death warrant.

The plots gave Protestant and Puritan MPs in parliament the opportunity to put pressure on Elizabeth to introduce stricter controls on Catholics. These are summarised in the box below.

Stricter controls on Catholics

- After the Ridolfi Plot, Elizabeth agreed to pass an Act saying that anyone who claimed she was not the rightful queen was a traitor.
- The fine for not attending a Protestant church service was raised to £20 per month (in 1559 it had only been 12 pence). Only the wealthiest Catholics could afford to pay such a large amount.
- Recusants who refused to pay their fines were imprisoned.
- A later law allowed the government to take two-thirds of the land of any recusant who had fallen behind with paying fines.
- In 1585, Catholic priests and Jesuits were given 40 days to leave England. If they did not, they would be tried for treason and executed.
- Anyone who offered shelter or help to a Catholic priest faced the death penalty. Soldiers could appear at any time to carry out a search of a Catholic house.
- Catholics over the age of 16 had to stay within five miles of their home at all times.
- Catholics were banned from holding large gatherings.

Torture and death

Torture was used more commonly than it had been during the reigns of previous kings and queens. The number of executions also increased. Elizabeth ordered the execution of at least 200 Catholics during her reign. Catholic priests were also executed as traitors. They were hanged, taken down and cut open while still conscious. Their internal organs were then taken out and burned in front of a large crowd. Parts of the body were often put on display as a warning to other Catholics who might follow their example and disobey the Queen.

◀ **SOURCE 1** This image comes from a book of Catholic propaganda that was published in Europe in 1587. It shows Margaret Clitherow being tortured. She was a butcher's wife in York. To avoid being executed, Margaret had refused to plead guilty or not guilty to an accusation that she had sheltered a Catholic priest. Her captors stretched Margaret out and placed a large, sharp stone beneath her back. A door was placed over her body and heavy weights were added on top. Margaret was crushed to death in her prison cell

Exam Tips

Show the sequence of events and highlight turning points

Use the Exam Tip on page 51 and advice below to help you answer this exam-style question. Remember to show the **sequence of events** that took place.

- In your first paragraph – you could explain why and how stricter controls and financial punishments were introduced against Catholics.
- In your second paragraph explain how and why stricter physical punishments were introduced.
- Demonstrate complex thinking by identifying key turning points that changed the way that Elizabeth and her government dealt with Catholics.

Apply Exam Practice

Question 3

Write an account of the ways in which Elizabeth's government dealt with the challenge of Catholicism. (8 marks)

6.6 The nature and ideas of the Puritans and Puritanism

Research & Record

How did Elizabeth respond to the Puritan challenge?

Read pages 74–5.

1. **Why** were Puritans unhappy with the Elizabethan Religious Settlement?
2. **How** did they complain and protest?
3. **How** did Elizabeth's government respond to Puritan protests?
4. **How far** did the Puritans represent a serious threat to Elizabeth? Explain your answer.

Puritan opposition to Elizabeth's Religious Settlement

Opposition to Elizabeth's Religious Settlement did not just come from Catholics. Puritans, with strict Protestant beliefs, thought that Elizabeth's religious policies did not go far enough to remove Catholic influences from the new Protestant Church. Elizabeth liked some of the old Catholic ways; she did not think that there was anything wrong with having some decorations in churches or priests wearing colourful robes. In contrast, Puritans wanted to 'purify' the church and remove all traces of the old Catholic religion. The diagram below summarises their beliefs.

How dangerous was the Puritan challenge?

There were many people in Elizabeth's court who were sympathetic to the Puritans, including key ministers such as Dudley and Walsingham. However, the Puritans were a relatively small group, based largely in London and the south-east of England. When some Puritans published pamphlets complaining about the Church and the bishops they lost a lot of support. Most people supported Elizabeth's Religious Settlement and the Church of England.

Ultimately, all Puritans agreed that it was better to have Elizabeth on the throne than the next in line, the Catholic, Mary Queen of Scots. Therefore, they did not lead rebellions or violent protests, or try to help a foreign power invade England.

Elizabeth's response to Puritan opposition

Elizabeth believed that her Religious Settlement was final. The Puritans should show loyalty rather than challenge her authority. Elizabeth did not want to get rid of bishops as they were part of the Church hierarchy which mirrored the social hierarchy (see page 33), with Elizabeth at the top.

Puritans who spoke out against her were dealt with harshly.

- Elizabeth stated that MPs were no longer allowed to discuss religious matters in Parliament without her permission. She imprisoned MPs who challenged her right to do this.
- When the Archbishop of Canterbury (Edmund Grindal) refused to close down Puritan prayer meetings, Elizabeth placed him under house arrest until his death. The new Archbishop expelled 200 Puritan priests for disobeying the rules of the Church.
- Puritan printing presses were destroyed. A Puritan called John Stubbs had his hand cut off for writing a pamphlet criticising Elizabeth for considering marriage to a French Catholic.

▲ **SOURCE 1** An illustration of John Stubbs' punishment from a *History of Britain*. It was published in 1923

Stubbs was then sent to prison. When he was released he became an MP and continued to criticise Elizabeth. However, he never argued that Elizabeth should be replaced by another monarch. His story shows how Puritans complained and criticised Elizabeth but never plotted to overthrow her.

Summarise

Look at the memory aid below. It summarises why the Catholics represented a **more** serious threat to Elizabeth than the Puritans. Write an explanation to prove each point.

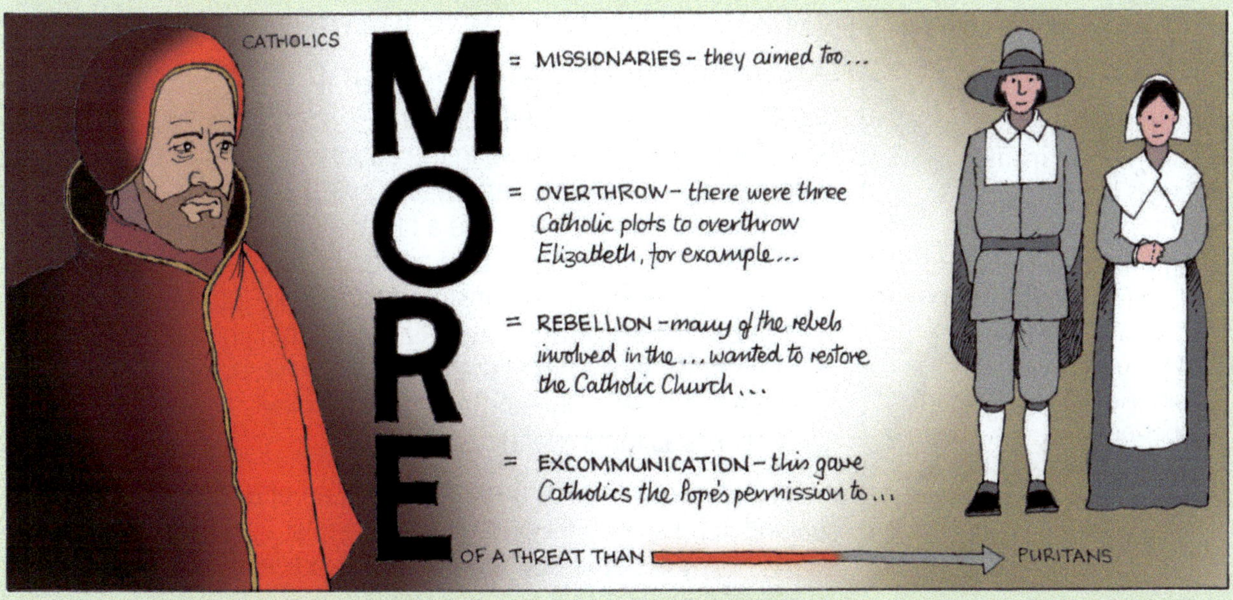

Topic 7 Mary Queen of Scots

7.1 The arrival of Mary Queen of Scots in England

Focus on ... Mary Queen of Scots

A thorn in Elizabeth's side

Mary Queen of Scots has already appeared quite a lot in this book. For much of Elizabeth's reign she seemed to be the person who would succeed to the throne if Elizabeth died without children. Parliament and Elizabeth's Privy Counsellors were worried that a Catholic could take over the country and put pressure on Elizabeth to marry.

In 1568, Mary's arrival in England created a real dilemma for Elizabeth. Part of her must have wanted to help a fellow queen and close relative (Elizabeth's father, Henry VIII had been Mary's great uncle). However, Mary proved to be a thorn in Elizabeth's side, causing quarrels with parliament and encouraging Elizabeth's enemies to plot against her.

To France ...

Mary had arrived in England via Scotland and France. Her father, King James V of Scotland, died when she was just six days old. Mary's mother (Mary of Guise) ruled the country until her daughter was old enough to make important decisions. Henry VIII was keen to gain control over Scotland and he soon put forward a plan for his son, Edward, to marry Mary Queen of Scots. But Mary of Guise was totally against this. She arranged for her daughter to marry the heir in the French throne instead.

An unhappy return to Scotland

Mary briefly became Queen of France but after her husband died she found herself unwanted in the country. She returned to Scotland where she married Lord Darnley, a young, handsome and ambitious Scottish lord. This proved to be a big mistake. Darnley wanted to rule Scotland himself and he plotted against his wife. One night in March 1566, Darnley and a group of supporters broke into Mary's room and seized her secretary, David Rizzio, stabbing him repeatedly before throwing him down the stairs. Mary was taken prisoner but managed to escape. In February 1567, Darnley's house was blown up and he was found dead nearby.

Mary's third marriage to the unpopular Earl of Bothwell angered leading Scottish nobles who rebelled against her. They defeated Mary's army in battle and forced her to abdicate. In 1568, Mary fled to England, hoping that Elizabeth would help her.

Reflect

Read page 76 and make links to what you have already studied. How many of the memory challenges below can you complete?

- Can you explain why Mary's religion and links with France would worry parliament?
- Can you explain how Mary was linked to the Northern Rebellion?
- Can you list three Catholic plots that Mary was involved in?

Elizabeth's dilemma

Research & Record

Why did the arrival of Mary Queen of Scots create a dilemma for Elizabeth?

The arrival of Mary Queen of Scots in England placed Elizabeth in a difficult position. She faced a real dilemma – should she help her cousin or view her as a dangerous threat? Read page 77. Explain the advantages and disadvantages of each of the options in a copy of the table.

Elizabeth's options	Advantages	Disadvantages
Let Mary go to France.	The French King had said that he would welcome her there.	France was Catholic and an old enemy of England – the French King could help Mary claim the English throne.
Send Mary back to Scotland.		
Let Mary live freely in England.		
Keep Mary prisoner in England.		
Execute Mary.		

1 If I die without children, Mary has the strongest claim to the English throne. But Mary is a strong Catholic – **if she becomes Queen of England she will turn England back to Catholicism.**

2 Mary is a female monarch who is the rightful ruler of Scotland. She has been forced to flee from Scotland after her lords rose up against her. **If she can be overthrown, it could happen to other female rulers – like me.**

3 **Mary has been accused of murdering her own husband.** My privy counsellors want the murder investigated.

4 Scotland is now a Protestant country run by powerful Scottish lords. We have an opportunity to **build a good relationship with Scotland.** If Mary returns to Scotland it could start a civil war.

5 **Mary's arrival has given English Catholics hope** and encouragement. They have already started causing trouble. There has been a rebellion in the north of England and the Ridolfi Plot. The Pope has excommunicated me and ordered English Catholics to disobey my laws.

6 **Parliament does not trust Mary.** They do not want her left free to cause trouble. Some MPs are demanding that Mary should be executed for stirring up rebellions and plots against me.

7 **I am worried about the threat from France and Spain.** These Catholic countries would love to stir up trouble in England and see me overthrown.

7.2 Elizabeth and parliament's treatment of Mary

Research & Record

How was Mary Queen of Scots treated in England?

Use the information on pages 78–9 and your knowledge of Mary Queen of Scots' background (see pages 76–7) to complete your own copy of this bingo card.

Mary Queen of Scots		
3 reasons why Mary was imprisoned	**3 plots** that Mary became involved in	**3 arguments** Mary used to defend herself at her trial
2 groups who wanted Mary imprisoned	**2 individuals** who supported plots to make Mary Queen	**2 countries** where Mary had been queen before she came to England
1 reason why Mary had a strong claim to the English throne	**1 individual** who found evidence of Mary's involvement in plots	**1 reason** why Elizabeth did not want to help Mary reclaim the Scottish throne

Reasons why Mary was imprisoned

When Mary fled to England she was convinced that Elizabeth would help her, but the support she hoped for never came. William Cecil argued that there should be an investigation into the rumours that Mary had been involved in the murder of her second husband. His aim was to keep her under guard for as long as possible.

Mary begged Elizabeth to allow her to live quietly in France but Elizabeth refused. Instead, Mary was locked up in an English castle where she was isolated and closely watched day and night. Mary remained a prisoner for nearly 20 years.

In all those years, Elizabeth refused to release or visit Mary, despite Mary's moving letters to her cousin.

There were a number of reasons why Elizabeth kept her prisoner so long. Look at the checklist opposite. How many of these reasons did you think of when you completed the task on page 77?

Mary's trial

After the Babington Plot, Elizabeth came under a lot of pressure from her Privy Council and parliament to execute Mary Queen of Scots. Elizabeth refused to agree to Mary's execution. She decided to put Mary on trial for treason.

Reasons to keep Mary in prison

- **Mary was a potential heir to the throne.** Since 1561, she had been displaying the English royal coat of arms to emphasise her claim to the English crown. This might not have been a problem, except for one very important issue – Mary was Catholic and England was now firmly a Protestant country.
- **Leaving Mary free could be dangerous.** Catholic plotters might group around her. Many Catholics in England and abroad believed that Elizabeth was illegitimate, the result of Henry VIII's illegal marriage to Anne Boleyn. They saw Mary Queen of Scots as the rightful Queen of England.
- **Helping Mary win back the Scottish throne would involve a costly war.** Elizabeth could not be sure that this campaign would be a success. William Cecil, her most trusted adviser, and the English Parliament were keen to support the Scottish Protestant Government of the Earl of Moray. William Cecil hated Mary Queen of Scots. He had sent money to the Earl of Moray to plot against Mary and remove her from power.

Summarise

The challenge posed by Mary

English Catholics had not caused Elizabeth major problems before Mary Queen of Scots arrived in England in 1568. Copy the table below and then use the knowledge you gained from Chapter 6 to fill in the second column to show how Mary quickly became the focus for Catholic plots against Elizabeth.

Plot	Explain what happened and Mary's involvement		The reaction from parliament and Privy Counsellors
Ridolfi		→	MPs demanded that Mary Queen of Scots should be executed. One MP called Mary 'the monstrous and huge dragon, the Queen of Scots'.
Throckmorton		→	Walsingham was determined to find clear proof that Mary was involved in the plots. He hired a double agent, who volunteered to take Mary's letters to France. Every message was opened and decoded.
Babington		→	Walsingham now had clear evidence that Mary had plotted to execute Elizabeth. He and Cecil demanded that Mary should be executed. Parliament agreed.

▲ **SOURCE 2** Mary Queen of Scots defends herself during her trial. From a history book published in 1920. On 12 October 1586, Mary was put on trial at Fotheringhay Castle in Northamptonshire. She defended herself during the trial, arguing that:

- God had made her Queen and no court had the right to try her. (Elizabeth secretly agreed with this.)
- The evidence could have been forged. (Historians think that some of it actually was.)
- The evidence of her involvement had been taken from Babington and others under torture.

Despite this strong defence, Mary was found guilty.

7.3 Mary's execution and its impact

Research & Record

What was the impact of Mary's execution?

1 Read pages 80–1. Explain why Elizabeth took so long to sign Mary's death warrant.

2 Did Mary's death increase or decrease the threat of Catholics plots and rebellions against Elizabeth? Explain your answer.

The death warrant

Despite the guilty verdict against Mary Queen of Scots, Elizabeth was reluctant to agree to her execution. She hated the idea of killing another queen, fearing that it could set a dangerous precedent and lead to other monarchs being executed. Parliament and the Privy Council insisted that Mary should be executed but it was not until February 1587 that Elizabeth changed her mind and finally signed the death warrant. This was after hearing rumours of Mary escaping and Spanish forces landing in Wales.

William Cecil made sure that the execution happened immediately, before Elizabeth had an opportunity to change her mind again. He and other Privy Counsellors persuaded Elizabeth's secretary, William Davison, to take the death warrant to Fotheringhay. It is said that Elizabeth was shocked and devastated to hear news of her cousin's execution.

The execution

Mary Queen of Scots was executed at Fotheringhay on 8 February 1587. She was led into the great hall of the castle where a crowd had gathered. Mary was wearing a black dress and a white veil over her hair. There were tears in her eyes when she sat on a stool and prayed in Latin.

Mary was blindfolded, knelt on a cushion and laid her head on the block. It took three blows to sever her head from her body. Immediately after the execution, a small dog was said to have crawled out from under Mary's petticoat, only to be dragged away. As the executioner went to hold up Mary's severed head, calling out 'God save the Queen' he made the mistake of grasping it by the hair. Mary was wearing a wig, and, to the shock of the crowd, Mary's skull fell to the ground and rolled across the floor.

Mary's prayer book, crucifix, blood-stained clothes and even the execution block were burned in the courtyard of the castle to make sure no relics remained. But her decaying body was left unburied until July 1587 when it was eventually taken to Peterborough Cathedral.

◀ **SOURCE 3** The execution of Mary Queen of Scots. A priest is holding a crucifix in front of Mary so that she can touch it as she dies

The consequences of the execution

Elizabeth's reaction

Elizabeth was furious when she heard the news that the death warrant had been sealed and sent to Fotheringhay. After the execution, Elizabeth claimed that she had given her secretary clear instructions not to have the death warrant sealed and argued that Davison and her advisers were to blame for the death of Mary Queen of Scots. She banned William Cecil from the royal court and refused to see him for six months while Davison was imprisoned in the Tower of London.

Reactions at home

In killing Mary, Elizabeth must have been worried that her cousin would become a martyr for the Catholic cause and that the execution could lead to English Catholics rising up in protest. However, this did not happen and there were no more Catholic plots for the rest of Elizabeth's reign.

Reactions abroad

Elizabeth was also worried that the death of Mary would cause anger abroad. However, England was already at war with Spain and although Mary's death angered Philip II, by this point he was already building his Armada in preparation for an invasion of England.

Some French Catholics demanded revenge for Mary's death, but the French King was worried about the growing power of Spain and the threat of civil war in France. He wanted to keep on friendly terms with Elizabeth and as a result did nothing.

James VI, King of Scotland, did protest at his mother's execution but Elizabeth was able to place the blame on her secretary and members of her Privy Council. James took no further action and eventually became King of England after Elizabeth's death in 1603. James had his mother's remains transferred from Peterborough Cathedral to Westminster Abbey, where a tomb was built. Mary Queen of Scots was buried opposite Elizabeth in the abbey. Mary's tomb was slightly bigger than Elizabeth's!

Apply Exam Practice

Question 2

Explain what was important about the arrival of Mary Queen of Scots in England. (8 marks)

Use the Exam Tips on pages 15, 31 and 63 to help you. Remember to plan your answer carefully. What big points are you going to build each of your two paragraphs around?

- Your first paragraph could explain how Mary's strong claim to the throne and religion created problems for Elizabeth.
- Your second paragraph could focus on Mary's involvement in plots against Elizabeth.

Summarise

The problems created by Mary Queen of Scots

Remember how the PERMS memory aid summarised the main problems Elizabeth faced.

This can also help you categorise the problems Mary Queen of Scots created for Elizabeth.

- What **p**olitical problems did Mary create? Think about the pressure Elizabeth faced (from parliament and even her own Privy Council) to deal with her harshly.
- What about Mary's **r**eligion and the way that complicated the **s**uccession?
- What about the **m**ilitary threat? Remember Mary and her family had close links with France.

POLITICAL problems – who was in charge
ECONOMIC problems – spending money wisely and not getting into debt
RELIGIOUS problems – whether England should by Protestant or Catholic
MILITARY problems – keeping safe against powerful enemies
SUCCESSION problems – producing an heir

Topic 8 The conflict with Spain

8.1 The reasons for conflict with Spain

Focus on ... Philip II

Ruler of an empire

Philip II became King of Spain in 1556. He ruled over a massive empire that included large areas of Europe, the Caribbean and South America. Philip was hardworking, loved reading books and was a dedicated Catholic. He saw it as his duty to serve God and he punished Protestants very severely. Philip was very suspicious of other people, finding it difficult to trust even his most faithful servants. Philip preferred to work alone and was known for taking a long time to reach decisions. Some of those decisions had a big impact on England.

Marriage to the English Queen

Even though Spain was Catholic, it had a good relationship with England before Elizabeth became Queen. Indeed, for a while, Philip was ruler of England too! Philip married the English Queen, Mary I in 1554 and his head appeared on English coins alongside Mary with a single crown above them. This was a symbol of joint rule. Mary even persuaded the Privy Council to send an English army to fight for Philip in his war against France.

After Mary's death, Elizabeth rejected Philip's marriage proposal and established a Protestant Church in England. However, Philip kept good relations with England. He was more worried about France, which he saw as Spain's most dangerous enemy.

Reflect

Read page 82.

1 Explain why Elizabeth rejected Philip's marriage proposal.
2 Give two examples of English sailors who attacked Spanish ships and settlements. Explain why Elizabeth supported these attacks.
3 List Catholic plots that Philip supported.

War with England

Over time, however, peaceful relations turned into rivalry as tensions grew between England and Spain. You have already learnt about some of the reasons why. Philip felt humiliated by English attacks on his treasure ships and Spanish settlements in the Caribbean and South America (see Chapter 5). Elizabeth was angered by Philip's involvement in Catholic plots to overthrow her, while he did not approve of the way that English Catholics were treated (see Chapter 6).

By the time of the execution of Mary Queen of Scots in 1587, Philip was already planning to invade England. As you will see on page 83, he saw Elizabeth's support for Dutch rebels in the Spanish Netherlands as an act of war. In 1588, Philip sent the Spanish Armada (a huge fleet of ships) to link up with his very best fighting troops in the Netherlands and invade England.

Research & Record

Why did tensions grow between England and Spain?

Use the knowledge you have gained from previous chapters and the information on pages 82–3 to explain why England and Spain came into conflict. Aim to write two paragraphs.

- In the first paragraph, focus on longer-term causes of the conflict. For example, Elizabeth's religious policies and Philip's support of Catholic plots.
- In your second paragraph focus on short-term causes. For example, problems caused by the rebellion in the Spanish Netherlands and English attacks on Spanish ships and settlements in Central and South America.

Causes of tension

Rebellion in the Netherlands

- When Protestants in the Netherlands rebelled against Spanish rule, Philip sent an army to crush the rebellion. The rebels were dealt with brutally by the Spanish army.
- Having such a strong army so close to England, and for the Netherlands to be so dominated by Spain were serious threats to Elizabeth.
- The rebellion affected England's economy. The cloth trade with Antwerp brought a lot of money into the country. Philip knew this and twice during the 1560s he banned English traders from Antwerp.

War between England and Spain

- Elizabeth sent money to help the Dutch rebels and allowed their ships to shelter in English ports. She also allowed English sailors to attack Spanish ships carrying supplies to the Netherlands.
- In 1584, a Catholic shot and killed Prince William of Orange, the leader of the Dutch Protestant rebels. This event shocked Elizabeth and pushed her into sending an army to help the Dutch rebels.
- In 1585, she signed the Treaty of Nonsuch with the Dutch rebels. England sent 7,000 soldiers, under the command of Robert Dudley, to the Netherlands. This boosted the morale of the Dutch rebels. However, Philip II saw the arrival of an English army in the Netherlands as an act of war against Spain.

▲ The areas of Europe controlled by Spain in the 1580s

Philip assembles a huge armada

- In 1585, Drake attacked towns controlled by Spain in the Caribbean. He returned to England with treasure worth £30,000. Angered by this and the arrival of English troops in the Netherlands, Philip planned to strike back. News soon reached England that Philip was assembling an armada (a great fleet of ships) that would invade England.
- Elizabeth started to strengthen England's defences. Each county was ordered to provide soldiers to defend the coast. Merchant ships that had been used for trade were converted into fighting ships. Warning beacons were set up around the coasts. Lookouts watched for the arrival of the Spanish boats.

8.2 Naval warfare – tactics and technology

Research & Record

How did the English forces compare to those of Spain?

Read pages 84–5.

1 Complete a table like this to compare English and Spanish forces using the criteria in the first column.
2 Use your table to identify two areas where the English had the advantage and two areas where the Spanish had the advantage.

Criteria	English forces	Spanish forces
Leadership and tactics		
Resources (ships, sailors and soldiers)		
Technology and weapons		

English Leadership

Lord Howard was a noble who had little experience of fighting at sea. However, his vice-admirals, Drake and Hawkins, were both very experienced.

versus

Spanish Leadership

The Duke of Medina Sidonia was brave and a good organiser but had little experience of sailing. However, his commanders were experienced sea captains. He was placed in charge of the Armada in February 1588, when the original commander died.

English tactics

- The aim was to destroy enemy ships at a distance by firing cannons at them.
- The English had more long-range guns than the Armada. These could be used to keep the Spanish at a safe distance and prevent them from using their favourite tactic of boarding their opponent's ships.

versus

Spanish tactics

- The intention was that the Armada would sail from Spain to the Netherlands where it would meet up with a large and experienced army led by Philip's best general, the Duke of Parma. The Armada would protect Parma's 27,000 troops as they crossed the Channel on barges (flat-bottomed boats) to land in Kent. A large Spanish army would then march towards London.
- When fighting at sea, the Spanish tactics were to get close to the enemy, and fire one round of cannon before ramming into the enemy ships. The Spanish would then use grappling hooks to attach themselves to the ships and then fight their way on to the ships and take them over.

English resources

- Elizabeth's annual income was around £300,000.
- The English forces were made up of 54 battleships which were strong, light and fast. Another 140 merchant ships were converted into battleships. This gave Elizabeth around 200 ships.
- There were 14,000 English sailors, the majority of whom were experienced.
- There were about 20,000 soldiers in England, but most of them had little training, few weapons and had to be spread along the coast. Elizabeth did not have the money to afford a large, professional army that could defend the country.

versus

Spanish resources

- Philip's annual income was £3 million.
- The Spanish Armada was made up of 130 ships armed with 2500 guns.
- The Armada had 64 battleships. Other ships carried supplies, but these ships were slow, heavy and difficult to handle in rough seas.
- There were 30,000 men on board the ships: 8000 experienced sailors, 19,000 well-trained solders and nearly 3000 servants.
- Another 27,000 experienced soldiers, led by the Duke of Parma, were waiting in the Netherlands.

English technology and weapons

The English fleet was strong. John Hawkins (see page 52), treasurer to the Navy, had spent many years improving the design of English ships. This meant that the fleet was manoeuvrable and well armed.

- English ships were lighter, faster and easier to manoeuvre than the Spanish ships.
- Hawkins had built a fleet of 24 newly designed 'race-built' warships – probably the best warships anywhere in the world.
- The English ships were about the same size as the Spanish ships, but could change direction quickly and had guns that could fire over a longer distance.
- The English forces had nearly 2000 cannon and smaller guns.
- The English cannons were light, and they could be fired quickly.
- They had 497 long-range guns and 251 medium-range guns.

versus

Spanish technology and weapons

- The Spanish had over 2400 guns – most of which could fire heavy cannon balls over a short distance.
- They had 172 long-range guns and 165 medium-range guns.
- The Spanish had plenty of ammunition (125,000 cannon balls) but they were not able to fire quickly enough. The design of the Spanish guns made them impossible to reload quickly. They were only able to fire one or two rounds a day.
- The Spanish cannon and cannon balls came from all over Europe; some of the cannon were badly made and many cannon balls did not fit the guns.
- The Spanish ships struggled to fire frequently and effectively.
- The ships were overall much slower and harder to manoeuvre than the English ships.

8.3 The Spanish Armada: key events

Research & Record

Where did the Spanish plan go wrong?

Read pages 86–7.

1. Identify three turning points when things went wrong for the Spanish.
2. Explain why each event had a negative impact on Spanish plans to invade England.

A = Armada assembled

B = Barges … to transport Alba's troops

C = Cadiz attacked

The Spanish plan

Philip II had a clear plan for invading England.

- The Armada would sail from Spain to Calais. It would meet up with a large and battle-hardened army from the Spanish Netherlands, led by Philip's best general, the Duke of Parma.
- The Armada would protect Parma's 27,000 troops as they crossed the Channel on barges.
- They would land in Kent. Spanish soldiers would march on London. Parma believed the crossing would take 12 hours and that his troops would take London within a week.
- They would then set up a temporary government, led by Cardinal Allen, the leader of the English Catholics who had been exiled from England. Philip hoped that English Catholics would rebel against Elizabeth and help the Spanish forces. The success of Philip's plan depended on good weather and precise timing.

April 1587: Drake's attack on Cadiz

- Elizabeth and her government knew about Philip's invasion plans. In April 1587, Francis Drake carried out a daring attack on the Spanish port of Cadiz. He destroyed 24 Spanish ships and many supplies.

The Armada is delayed

- Drake then headed for the Azores where he planned to capture Spanish treasure ships returning from India and America. The Spanish sent a fleet to protect their treasure ships which further delayed their invasion plans. Drake's actions gave the English another year to prepare for Philip's invasion.

D = Delay

29 July 1588: The Armada sails into the English Channel

- The Spanish Armada sailed into the English Channel in crescent formation.
- The English fleet chased after them using their long-distance cannon to fire at the Spanish fleet. They did not cause serious damage. The Spanish only lost three ships.

E = English Channel

6–7 August: Fireships spread panic

- The Armada reached Calais on 6 August. The Duke of Parma sent a message to Medina Sidonia that he and his troops were only 50 km away, but they were being attacked by the Dutch. Parma said it would take them a week to reach Calais.
- Lord Howard did not know that Parma's troops were held up so during the night he decided to take action. He filled eight unmanned ships with tar, gunpowder and other inflammable materials. Shortly after midnight on 7 August these ships were set alight and let loose to drift into Calais harbour.
- The Spanish sailors panicked when they saw the English fireships. They cut anchor and sailed out of the protection of the harbour. The Spanish fleet was scattered and blown by strong winds towards sandbanks off the coast of the Netherlands.

F = Fireships

8 August: The Battle of Gravelines

- At daylight on 8 August, Lord Howard ordered the English ships to attack. The English now had the wind and the currents in their favour. For nine hours, they launched a ferocious and relentless attack on the Armada. This was called the Battle of Gravelines.
- The battle was fought in rough seas. This suited the English ships, which were lighter and easier to manoeuvre in bad weather.
- The English guns could be reloaded quickly and their close-range cannon fire badly damaged many Spanish ships. In contrast, the Spanish guns could not reload quickly. No English ships suffered major damage.
- Although much of the battle was fought at close-quarters, the English were careful not to let the Spanish close enough to use their grappling irons to board English ships.
- A total of 1000 Spanish sailors were killed and about 800 were wounded but only 50 English sailors were killed. The battle ended when the English fleet ran out of ammunition.

G = Gravelines

8.4 The defeat of the Spanish Armada

Research & Record

Why was the Spanish Armada defeated?

1 Read pages 88–9. Use this information and what you have already found out from pages 84–7 to fill in a copy of the table.

2 Which factor do you think played the most important role in the defeat of the Spanish Armada?

Identify – What factors led to the defeat of the Armada?	Examples – When did this factor play an important role?	Explanation – Why was this important? What happened as a result?
Luck	The Battle of Gravelines was fought in bad weather.	This gave the English an advantage as their ships were easier to manoeuvre in stormy seas.
Effective English tactics		
Spanish mistakes		
Technology (English advantages)		

H = Horrendous storms – drive the Armada north

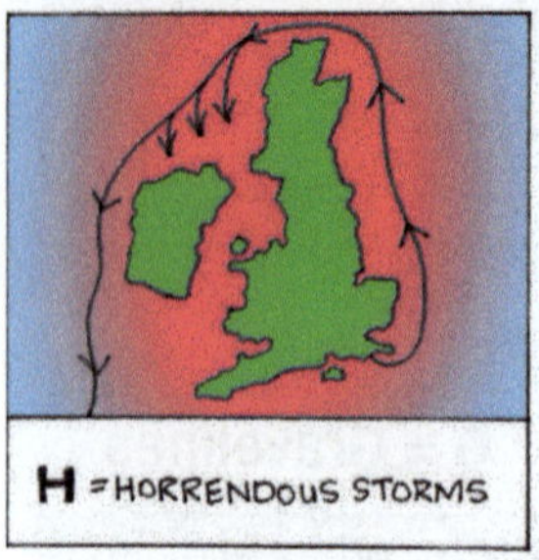

9 August: The Armada is forced north

- On 9 August the wind changed direction, making it impossible for the Spanish to fight their way back into the English Channel. The Armada was forced to sail into the North Sea.
- The English fleet chased after it for two days until the Armada sailed past the Scottish border. By this time the English were short of ammunition and food. Many sailors were sick. The boats turned back and headed south.
- Elizabeth and her government still feared that the Duke of Parma might attack. Elizabeth travelled to Tilbury in Essex where 4000 soldiers were guarding the coast. It was here, dressed in armour and on horseback, that she gave a famous, rousing speech to raise the morale of her troops.

Let tyrants fear. I have always … placed my chiefest strength and safeguard in the loyal hearts and goodwill of my subjects. Therefore I am amongst you, … at this time, not for my recreation and disport, but being resolved, in the midst and heat of battle, to live and die amongst you all ….

I know I have the body of a weak and feeble woman; but I have the heart and stomach of a king, and a king of England too, and think foul scorn that Parma or Spain, or any prince of Europe, should dare to invade the borders of my realm.

September–October: Storms destroy the Armada

- The Armada carried on around Scotland and Ireland. The Spanish sailors had not sailed this route before. They did not have accurate maps and their supplies were running low. Many men became sick from having to drink polluted water and eat rotten food.
- To make matters worse, gales and strong winds drove many Spanish ships on to the rocks off the coasts of Scotland and Ireland. Thousands of sailors drowned or were killed by the local population when they struggled ashore.
- The Spanish lost over 50 ships, most of which were destroyed on this journey around Scotland and Ireland (only five were captured or sunk by the English Navy). Only 80 ships made it back to Spain. A total of 20,000 Spanish sailors and soldiers were killed.

I = Ireland … many ships destroyed

Apply ▶ Exam Practice

Question 1

Study Interpretation A. How convincing is Interpretation A about the reasons for the defeat of the Spanish Armada? Explain your answer using Interpretation A and your contextual knowledge. (8 marks)

▼ **Interpretation A** – Dan Snow (an extract from an article in *BBC History* magazine)

There were huge flaws in the entire invasion plan. It was simply unworkable. The fleet was meant to meet up with the Duke of Parma – who was commanding Spanish forces in the Netherlands – before loading men onto the ships and continuing to England, where the recently boosted army would then launch an invasion. But for various technical reasons – tides, timings and the boats themselves – that plan could never have worked. The Spanish were sailing up the Channel with the utmost guarantee of failure.

The Spanish Armada was catastrophically defeated at the Battle of Gravelines. After the battle, the damaged Spanish fleet was driven towards the shallows off the coast of the Netherlands, but a change in wind direction actually enabled it to limp off into the North Sea, away from the English navy. It was only as the remains of the Armada sailed around northern Scotland and past the east coast of Ireland that it was battered by the elements. Any strategic threat the Spanish fleet had posed to the English throne had already been destroyed at Gravelines.

Exam Tip

Use the advice on page 63 to help you answer the exam question.

- How far do you agree that the Spanish plan was poorly thought through?
- How far do you agree that the Battle of Gravelines was a crucial turning point?

8.5 The consequences of the defeat of the Spanish Armada

Research & Record

Why was the defeat of the Spanish Armada important?

Use pages 90–1 to help you fill in your copy of the table and explain why the defeat of the Armada had important consequences for England.

Consequences	Explanation
Political	The defeat of the Armada was a propaganda boost because …
Economic	The high cost of war led to …
Religious – England remained Protestant	Had the Armada succeeded, it is likely that …
Military – England was made more secure from invasion	This was because …
Military – many English sailors died	This was a result of …

Impact on the sailors

Only around 80 ships made it back to Spain. The Spanish lost 20,000 men in their failed invasion. However, thousands of English sailors died too and mostly not in battle. After the Battle of Gravelines they were kept on board ships for weeks because Elizabeth could not afford to pay them. Many died of hunger or disease in filthy and overcrowded conditions. Many never got to celebrate the famous victory over the Spanish Armada.

Impact on the Netherlands

The northern part of the Netherlands became independent which benefited English trade and helped to make England more secure from invasion. The southern area of the Netherlands remained in Spanish control.

Impact on Philip's invasion plans

Philip did not give up his invasion plans following the defeat of the Armada. He sent two more armadas to invade England (in 1596 and 1597). Luckily for Elizabeth both were wrecked by storms.

In 1601, a Spanish army did land in Ireland in support of Catholic rebels. The Spanish hoped to create a base there for a future invasion of England but the Spanish army was defeated and the Irish rebellion ended in 1603.

It was not until after Elizabeth's death that the war with Spain finally ended. In 1604, the Treaty of London ended the war between England and Spain that had lasted for almost 20 years.

The impact on England

The defeat of the Spanish Armada stopped an invasion of England. If Medina Sidonia had managed to escort the Duke of Parma's 27,000-strong invasion army to the English coast it is probable that they would have defeated Elizabeth's much smaller army, captured London and re-introduced Catholicism.

The war with Spain also changed English attitudes towards Catholics. Strict laws were introduced against them (see page 72). They were treated with suspicion and seen as dangerous people who were a real threat to the safety of the English monarchy.

The war against Spain put a lot of pressure on the English economy, increasing taxes and causing **inflation** and hardship for the poor.

On the positive side, the defeat of the Armada was a huge propaganda boost for Elizabeth and it raised morale in the country and national pride. The role played by the wind was taken as a sign of God's approval of Protestantism in England.

◀ **SOURCE 1** The Silver Victory medal that Elizabeth gave to her admirals after the defeat of the Spanish Armada. The caption around the image says, 'God blew and they (the Spanish fleet) were scattered.'

Summarise

Look at the **4 Rs** memory aid that we have produced to help you remember the reasons that Philip II had for attempting to invade England.

Create your own memory aid that helps you remember the consequences of the defeat of the Spanish Armada. You could produce a diagram or an image. Try to get across the positive results **and** the problems that continued.

Apply Exam Practice

Question 4

'Luck was the main reason for the outcome of naval battles in Elizabethan times.' How far does a study of the defeat of the Spanish Armada support this statement? (16 marks)

Exam Tips

Develop your explanations so that you prove the importance of factors

Use the table you produced (see page 88) and the advice on page 45 to help you plan your answer. Remember to deal with the reason/factor given in the question in your first paragraph. Then compare the relative importance of two other factors before reaching a clear judgement. Look at the paragraph below. It models how you can prove the importance of a factor.

*In the second and third sentences, two pieces of evidence are provided to **support** this argument.*

*The last two sentences provide an **explanation** of why the factor was so important. Connectives such as 'without', 'meant that' and 'this resulted in', combined with good knowledge can help you prove importance.*

> Superior English technology played an essential role in the defeat of the Spanish Armada. John Hawkins had helped to design English battleships that were faster and easier to manoeuvre than the Spanish ships. Moreover, the English cannon were quick to reload. In contrast, some of the Spanish cannon balls did not fit their guns and they struggled to fire more than one round. Without these technological advantages the English Navy may not have been able to win the Battle of Gravelines. Better designed ships and weapons meant that they were able to damage many Spanish ships through close-range cannon fire.

*The first sentence makes the **argument clear** – the factor was 'essential'.*

*In the fourth sentence, specific **comparisons** are made to further support the argument.*

Part 3: Troubles at home and abroad review

Review 1

A Golden Age?

On page 62 you evaluated how far Elizabeth's reign should be seen as a Golden Age. This was based on your study of Chapters 3, 4 and 5. Now that you have studied the last three chapters of this book, how has your view changed? Do Elizabeth's religious policies, her treatment of Mary Queen of Scots and the conflict with Spain support or challenge the idea of a Golden Age?

Look at the argument below and complete the ABC challenge opposite.

The Elizabethan period should be seen as a Golden Age. There was a growth in prosperity and **culture** flourished. Living standards improved and houses became more comfortable to live in. This was definitely a Golden Age for the theatre and sailors established new trading routes.

Elizabeth faced a number of challenges to her authority, yet she was able to create a period of peace and stability at home, as well as dealing with threats from abroad. She introduced a Religious Settlement that was accepted by most of the population.

The ABC challenge

A = Add 'killer evidence' to support the claim made in the argument. Which groups grew more prosperous? How did houses become more comfortable? Give examples of new trading routes.

B = Build an even stronger argument. Explain how and why the theatre became more popular. Explain the importance of the new trade links.

C = Challenge the idea of a Golden Age. Did everyone become more prosperous and benefit from improved living conditions? Explain why some people faced imprisonment or even torture because of their religious beliefs. Explain how war with Spain continued even after the defeat of the Armada.

Review 2

Who was Elizabeth's most important minister?

Look at this contemporary drawing of Elizabeth I flanked by William Cecil (Lord Burghley) and Sir Francis Walsingham. Do you think that these two men were her most important ministers?

- What positions did they have in Elizabeth's government? Why were these important?
- Who could Elizabeth trust for advice?
- Who helped to uncover plots against her?

Review 3

Look at the images below.

Can you place these in chronological order to tell the story of the Spanish Armada?

Use the A–I memory aid to write a short label for each image. You can check your answer by referring to pages 86–9.

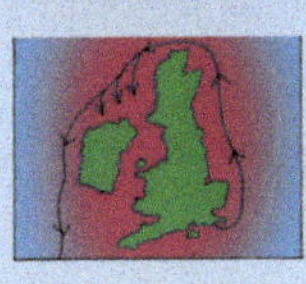

Apply Exam Practice

Here is a full set of exam-style questions covering the whole course. Use the Exam Tips throughout the book to help you answer each type of question.

Question 1

Study Interpretation A. How convincing is Interpretation A about the reasons for the defeat of the Spanish Armada? Explain your answer using Interpretation A and your contextual knowledge. (8 marks)

▼ **Interpretation A** – Robert Hutchinson (an extract from an article in *BBC History* magazine)

It was bad luck, bad tactics and bad weather that defeated the Spanish Armada – not the derring-do displayed on the high seas by Elizabeth's intrepid sea dogs …

Only six Spanish ships out of the 129 that sailed against England were destroyed as a direct result of naval combat. However, a minimum of 50 Armada ships (probably as many as 64) were lost through accident or during the Atlantic storms that scattered the fleet en route to England and as it limped, badly battered, back to northern Spain.

More than 13,500 sailors and soldiers did not come home – the vast majority victims not of English cannon fire, but of lack of food and water, virulent disease and incompetent organisation.

Question 2

Explain what was important about the problem of poverty in Elizabethan England. (8 marks)

Question 3

Write an account of the ways in which the Puritans challenged Elizabeth's Religious Settlement. (8 marks)

Question 4

The main change that the homes of the Elizabethan gentry demonstrated was the greater prosperity of their owners. How far does a study of Hardwick Hall support this statement? Explain your answer. You should refer to Hardwick Hall and your contextual knowledge. (16 marks)

Glossary

Revision Tip

This glossary is not just for looking up meanings. You can use it interactively to test yourself regularly. For example:

1. Ask someone to read out a definition and see if you can guess the key term.
2. Ask someone to read out a key term and see if you can explain to them what the key term means. If possible, aim to give an example to support your definition.
3. For the **KEY INDIVIDUALS** – identified in red – aim to:
   - Identify when and why they were important.
   - Link them to the key events.
4. For the **KEY EVENTS** – identified in blue – make sure you can:
   - State when the event occurred.
   - Explain the causes of the event. For an extra challenge, can you categorise these into short-/long-term causes and/or political/economic/religious causes?
   - Explain the consequences of the event. What was the immediate/short-term impact of the event? What were the longer-term consequences?

ALMSHOUSES places that provided food, clothing and shelter to the 'impotent poor'

ARMADA naval fleet or group of warships – in the Elizabethan era this refers to the **SPANISH ARMADA** and the attempt to invade England

BABINGTON PLOT a Catholic plot to murder Elizabeth and make Mary Queen of Scots the new Queen of England, partly organised by Anthony Babington

CATHOLIC a member of the Roman Catholic Church, led by the Pope

CECIL, WILLIAM (later became Lord Burghley) Elizabeth's Secretary of State and most trusted adviser (1558–72 and 1590–98)

CENSORSHIP stopping people accessing information and ideas that a ruler or government does not want them to read, see or hear

CIRCUMNAVIGATION sailing around the circumference of the world

COLONY an area under the control of another country

COURT the group of people who gathered around the Queen wherever she was (included advisers, key ministers, officials and servants)

COURTIER member of the court

CULTURE the ideas, customs and social behaviour of people in a society

DUDLEY, ROBERT (later became the Earl of Leicester) a close childhood friend of Elizabeth's who became an important member of her Privy Council

DRAKE, FRANCIS English sailor who circumnavigated the world, attacked Spanish treasure ships and played an important role in the defeat of the Spanish Armada

ELIZABETHAN RELIGIOUS SETTLEMENT established a Protestant Church of England, with Elizabeth as its Supreme Governor

EMPIRE a group of colonies or areas of land ruled by a single more powerful country

ESSEX, THE EARL OF a member of Elizabeth's Privy Council and one of her favourite courtiers and key ministers. Rebelled against Elizabeth in 1601 in what was known as **ESSEX'S REBELLION**

EXCOMMUNICATION to be expelled from the Catholic Church. **ELIZABETH I'S EXCOMMUNICATION** was ordered by the Pope in 1570

GENTRY landowners who grew in wealth and influence during the Elizabethan period but did not have titles (so they were below the rank of the nobility)

HAWKINS, JOHN English sailor who traded in enslaved people and designed ships

HIERARCHY a system by which people were organised in different layers of importance

HOUSES OF CORRECTION places where the 'idle poor' or beggars were imprisoned

IMPOTENT POOR people unable to work and look after themselves

INFLATION rising prices

LIVING STANDARDS the quality of housing, living conditions and wealth experienced by an individual or group

JESUIT Roman Catholic missionary priests who wanted to convert people to Catholicism

JUSTICES OF THE PEACE (JPs) kept law and order in a district/area and carried out the orders of the Privy Council

LORD LIEUTENANTS responsible for governing a county for the monarch and for organising an army from the county to fight for the country during a time of war

MARY I Elizabeth's half-sister. Ruled England 1553–58. She was a Catholic who restored the authority of the Pope

MARY QUEEN OF SCOTS The Catholic Queen of Scotland who fled to England in 1568. As long as Elizabeth remained childless, she was the heir to the English throne

MINISTER appointed by Elizabeth to help her run the country

MISSIONARIES sent to England to persuade people to follow the Catholic religion

MONOPOLY a licence, granted by the monarch, that gave an individual or group the right to sell a product

NEW WORLD The name used in the Elizabethan era for North and South America

NOBLES Wealthy and powerful men who owned large areas of land

NORFOLK, THE DUKE OF also known as Thomas Howard, the Fourth Duke of Norfolk. Executed for his role in the Ridolfi Plot

NORTHERN REBELLION A rebellion in the north of England led by the Earls of Northumberland and Westmorland

PAPAL BULL a document or instruction issued by the Pope

PARLIAMENT called by Elizabeth when she needed to pass laws or raise taxes. MPs were nominated by nobles or the monarch and sat in the House of Commons. Nobles sat in the House of Lords

PATRONAGE using your wealth, power and influence to reward others in return for loyalty and support

PHILIP II King of Spain, also married to Mary I

PLAGUE an infectious disease. Bubonic plague was spread to humans by fleas from rats; pneumonic plague was spread by people coughing

POOR LAWS laws that established how poor people were to be treated in Tudor times

POVERTY being poor and not having enough money for adequate food, shelter and living conditions

PROGRESSES when the monarch toured the country staying at the homes of the nobility

PRIVY COUNCIL the group of key ministers who advised Elizabeth

PROPAGANDA spreading ideas that are designed to persuade people to think or behave in a certain way

PURITAN someone who holds extreme Protestant views and is strongly opposed to the Catholic religion and its forms of worship

RALEIGH, WALTER English sailor and one of Elizabeth's favourite courtiers

RECUSANTS Catholics who refused to go to Protestant church services

RIDOLFI PLOT a Catholic plot to overthrow Elizabeth, make Mary Queen of Scots the new Queen and marry her to the Duke of Norfolk

SECRETARY OF STATE the most important minister within the Privy Council

SUCCESSION the arrangement of who should take over from a monarch after they die

THROCKMORTON PLOT a Catholic plot to free Mary Queen of Scots and restore Catholicism and a Catholic monarchy, partly organised by Francis Throckmorton

TREASON disloyalty to the monarch

VAGABOND (OR VAGRANT) a homeless, unemployed person who traveled from place to place looking for work

WALSINGHAM, FRANCIS Elizabeth's Secretary of State (1572–90); helped to organise a spy network that uncovered Catholic plots against Elizabeth

YEOMEN farmers who owned their own land

Index